# MARY *o...*

JENNY ROBERTSON has written a number of books, Bible stories and Bible reading notes. Her books published by Triangle include *Praying with the English Mystics*, and *The Uninvited Guest*, a personal journey through her daughter's severe schizophrenia. *Don't Go to Uncle's Wedding* (published by Azure) tells the story of the Warsaw Ghetto. Jenny has lived in Russia and had contact with Russian Orthodoxy. She now lives in Poland where her husband is Anglican Chaplain. Many of her personal interests and spirituality have come together in *Mary of Nazareth*.

# MARY *of* NAZARETH

### JENNY ROBERTSON

TRIANGLE

Published in Great Britain in 2001
Triangle
SPCK
Holy Trinity Church
Marylebone Road
London NW1 4DU

British Library Cataloguing-in-Publication Data

A catalogue record for this book is available from
the British Library

ISBN 0-281-05390-1

Typeset by Pioneer Associates, Perthshire
Printed in Great Britain by
Omnia Books, Glasgow

*To Xanthe*

# *Contents*

———◆———

# *Acknowledgements*

———◆———

All Bible quotations are from the New King James Version, except where stated.

The poems on pages xiii–xiv and 116 and the translations of poems on pages 47 and 109 are by the author.

The author and publishers would like to thank Father Aidan Doherty for his poem 'Joseph'.

'The Art of Blessing the Day' by Marge Piercy is reproduced with permission from Five Leaves Publications.

# Mary of Nazareth – a journey into unconditional love

This book has been simmering for a long time. There have been many steps on the way and I invite you to accompany me as we explore the role of Mary of Nazareth in the Christian story. The young unmarried girl who became the mother of the Lord Jesus is a positive role model for women and men in our journey to God. Her place in Scripture repays further study. It highlights the inter-weaving of faith and challenge, blessing and promise, in God's great love letter to all people. Mary, the mother of the Lord, provides an almost inexhaustible aid to meditation and contemplation.

Many strands of biblical thought are woven into the first two chapters of Luke's Gospel, in which we meet Mary as a daughter of Israel who embodies the courage and passion of the great forebears of faith. Mary has her place in the coming of Christ (he could not have come without her). A prophet in her own right, she looks forward to the new covenant, brings the Lord of the covenant to birth and nurtures him. She also belongs to the 'humble poor', whose faithful waiting prepared the way for the Messiah. Luke's Gospel gives us fascinating portraits of Mary and Joseph, Elizabeth and Zechariah, Simeon and Anna. They are all people so pregnant with hope that they, in a faith-sense, 'birthed' the Messiah, as we must do repeatedly all through our Christian experience.

Tucked in between the books of Habakkuk and Haggai are the words of the prophet Zephaniah:

> The LORD says: 'I will leave in your midst a meek and humble people, and they shall trust in the name of the LORD . . . Sing, O daughter of Zion . . . Be glad and rejoice with all your heart, O daughter of Jerusalem . . . The LORD your God in your midst, the Mighty One, will save; he will rejoice over you with gladness; he will quiet you in his love, he will rejoice over you with singing.' (Zephaniah 3.12, 14, 17)

Mary fulfils this prophecy exactly. She is 'meek and humble' – and she is strong in trust and joy. She knows herself to be blessed above all other women and she is confident that the Lord, 'the Mighty One, will save'. She stakes her whole life on that great truth. She is ready to face shame and scandal. She rejoices in the Lord – but she has to reach the point where the Lord rejoices over her. Mary has to learn to 'let go and let God', not just once, when the angel came, but many times. She holds the infant Christ in her arms; she quiets him with her love; but her path, like our own, leads to Calvary, until she reaches the place where God comforts her at the foot of the cross. She must allow her God to 'quiet her with his love'. She allows John the beloved disciple to lead her into a new faith-family – which will nurture her towards Easter and Pentecost. Hers is a multifaceted role within the drama of faith.

Mary's Magnificat is a radiant affirmation of God, of the

covenant and of the very essence of the Gospels. It is a link between the faith-world of the Old Testament and that of the New. When Mary sings, 'He has filled the hungry with good things, and the rich he has sent away empty' (Luke 1.53), she is voicing the astonishing truth which her son will proclaim in the Beatitudes. This is the great mystery of God's 'bias to the poor', which produced such lasting fruit in the lives of great saints like Francis of Assisi and Mother Teresa – and which challenges and provokes us all.

These ideas form the basis of a poem which will be woven through the book:

### Mary's Song

The commonplace makes a music of its own:
water sparkles – a summer song,
with flash of dove wings over Nazareth.
A cloud lingers
and dove and sun and song are gone.

'Don't speak of love,' a woman whispered,
'it vanishes when troubles come.'

I'll speak instead of poppies in scarlet dress,
bending as the wind directs;
of sickles scything pliant corn;
of wine and oil:
seepings of vat and press.

My first-born works with wood. I curl
fragile tissue, soft as hay
between my fingers; marvel

that mast and plough are made
from this felled and damaged tree
whose canticle awoke the sun.

Now wood and worker, wound and world are one.

## Mary the disciple – an example for all Christians

Mary the mother shared her son's hidden life. Her part in the Christian story points up qualities of mercy and interior stillness. From her we learn the spirituality of motherhood – in its broadest, least physical sense as well as its more obvious one. Like Peter, like Paul, Mary the disciple is an example for all Christians. She belongs to the nitty-gritty of everyday life, not to the stained-glass window or the Christmas card.

A true understanding of Mary will always show her pointing away from herself and towards her son. Thinking this through I began to understand the sources of a more contemplative form of prayer, which rejoices in the everyday because 'wood and worker, wound and world are one'. This kind of prayer gives permission for things to be as they are – and this is something I personally struggle with. Mary's faith, her song and her life in the Gospels teach me that the incarnation has brought our human effort and achievement, as well as our brokenness and hurt, into a deep unity with the creator of all.

As we follow Mary through the pages of the Gospels, we shall see that the young woman whose position and place in the Church has so often divided Christians can become a source of reconciliation. The mother who has seemed to separate us may finally unite us. I was moved recently when a Muslim friend spoke very respectfully of Mary, the mother of Jesus. 'We call her Bibi Mariam,' she explained. 'Bibi is a title of honour and Mariam is the Arabic for Mary.' Can Bibi Mariam draw people of goodwill of all faiths more generously together?

## Miriam, village girl and teenage mother of a gifted child

Well, Mariam, yes; but how about Miriam, the village girl, growing up in Nazareth? Her hands were capable and strong. She could cook and weave. She carried water from the well. She became the teenage mother of a gifted child. She knew doubt and sorrow, yet she was there when he died, standing with him at the cross.

Pope John Paul II has called her 'Virgin Saint Mary, Mother of Beautiful Love'. I saw the outworking of this concept at a gathering in eastern Poland. Crowds had come from Belarus, from the Ukraine, as well as from Poland. After the Pope's address, people from all walks of life climbed a long flight of carpeted steps with gifts for the Pope.

One woman carried something that looked like a large doll. Slowly she mounted the steps – they seemed endless to me as I watched. I couldn't see what was in the bundle she bore, but my husband was in the delegation on the platform and he saw and told me. The woman bore an armless, legless child, a girl. Remember, this was eastern Poland and the contaminated cloud from Chernobyl had passed over this region in 1986.

So the woman came to the Pope with her daughter. She

knelt and he bent forward and tenderly stroked her cheek and the face of her child. Her audience with him lasted longer than anyone else's that day, and he blessed the maimed being she bore.

And for me this was an icon: an icon of courage, hope and compassion which surely embodied Mary of Nazareth, who had watched the naked body of her son, 'without form or comeliness', be taken from the cross and be borne away to a borrowed grave.

I saw acceptance and unconditional love: the total love of a mother for a damaged child. The greed and deceit of a pitiless power had created the Chernobyl disaster, which deformed an unborn daughter in her mother's womb. The mother's love turned that tragedy into triumph, not of the body, but of the heart. I stored the memory away. It seemed an important signpost on my quest.

A few months later, I watched a film made in 1994 by a Macedonian director, Milczo Manczewski. It had won the Golden Lion in Venice and had been voted 'best film' in the Warsaw Film Festival. Shot on location in Macedonia, it was beautiful, mysterious and cruel. The countryside of Macedonia was as harsh as the lives of its people, who sheltered in hovels of stone with roughly thatched roofs – and lived in fear of Albanian guerrillas. Blood demanded blood – and yet there was unsurpassed beauty in the land- scape, a raw humour in the lives of the people, self-sacrifice and love, made more poignant by the death all around.

The film, inevitably, was interspersed with advertisements for deodorant, soap powder, smart cars. Nothing could have contrasted more. On the one hand was the world of superficial gloss and comfort, on the other were oxen dragging a rough plough over dry, stony soil; a woman riding side-saddle on a donkey she beat with a length of rope; twin lambs being born; the ancient Slavonic chanting of monks; men knocking back drink – and the sound of machine gunfire ripping through flesh.

And yet, which world is the more real?

Into the film came a young widow, an Albanian, secluded, shrouded in a short black scarf bound low on her forehead and across her chin. The film turned upon the moment when this woman in the mountains came by night to a man who had returned to the village. She came into his bedroom, but not into his bed. 'Help me. My child is lost,' she said.

And I thought: Miriam of Nazareth must have been like that young widow seeking her lost child. No flaxen Madonna in mantle of blue, but a woman of her time and place – a time and place I can imagine by reading background books, but in which I would struggle to survive. And how would we understand each other's language?

We would understand sorrow, we would understand joy. We would understand silence and we would understand loss. We would understand the birth of twin lambs, wriggling blind and wet on to wobbly feet. We would understand the flow of water for thirst and for cleansing, the flame beneath the cooking pot, the smell of food for our hunger. We would understand the way the whole of creation has been permeated by the Godhead, not just the beautiful things, but the messy parts as well. We would understand bereavement, yes, and we would understand the need for life to go on. Jesus understood it too. He saw his mother at the foot of the cross and he gave her into the keeping of John, the beloved follower. 'Woman, behold your son. Son, behold your mother.' But in giving mother

Mary to the apostle John, the Lord was giving her to the Church, to all of us. He gave her as mother, a widow-mother from a village. And this is how I saw her, a mother in the black scarf of widowhood in a small village in the mountains of a Europe I have never entered. I understood that this was for real. Because where there is physical poverty but spiritual wealth, where there is a 'meek and humble people' who 'trust in the name of the Lord', the Mighty One will save, as he promises in the words of Zephaniah. He will rejoice with gladness and with singing and he will quiet each of these humble ones with his love.

This is the spiritual legacy of Mary of Nazareth. Let us hear her confident acclamation of joy, let us accompany her into the holiness of knowing and affirming that we are blessed, into the quietness of being unconditionally loved.

## To ponder

A true understanding of Mary will always show her pointing away from herself and towards her son. Do you see a role model here for yourself and for the Church? As we journey through this book, hold on to ways in which understanding Mary may help us to find common ground with other Christians and between those of other faiths.

# CHAPTER 1

## *The music of the everyday*

———◆———

Mary of Nazareth is a woman who is chosen – and who accepts God's challenge. She is a prophet whose words bridge the Old Testament and the New; a woman of faith who at one point fails to recognize the implications of her son's life and teachings, but who follows him to the foot of the cross – and beyond, into the new Spirit-filled life of the Church.

In Mary's pregnancy, her delivery, her flight and her return to her humble home in Nazareth, the great gospel truth is realized: the commonplace is the place where God encounters us. This is why 'the commonplace makes a music of its own'. Hearing the music of the everyday helps us to pray within the context of daily life, hallowing it and making it the place where God can work.

For example, a friend of mine mentioned that she keeps a list of six prisoners on death row beside a picture of the holy mother and child. Every day she covers the list of names and the picture with her hand and prays the *Ave Maria* and the Jesus Prayer for those condemned to die, bringing them into the loving circle of the mother and child by touch and by the use of prayers rooted in Scripture.

The picture she uses had come from Russia. One Russian Christmas Eve (6 January), a group of St Petersburg schoolchildren, mums and teachers and I walked across the massively frozen River Volga to visit a monastery. It had been desecrated by the communists and was being gradually restored. As young girls dressed in black robes busily brushed away copious dollops of hardened candle grease, I bought a small icon of the virgin mother and child – and later gave it to my friend. It was lovely to think that a tiny icon from that monastery beside the frozen Volga might be used as a living link in prayer. It is so easy to promise to pray, and then to give up because it's hard to find the right words. Yet here, as so often, 'actions speak louder than words'. The apostle Paul advises us to use our bodies in worship. 'Offer yourselves to God, as those who have been brought from death to life; and offer the parts of your body to him as instruments of righteousness' (Romans 6.13).

As we saw, a true understanding of Mary will always show her pointing away from herself and towards her son; and indeed, this is exactly how she is depicted in Eastern Orthodox icons. The greatest of these show her as the Virgin of Tenderness, whose limitless sorrow is shown in her huge eyes. The mother is shown as a throne on which her infant son is elevated and from which he blesses the world. These icons compel the onlooker to contemplate the mystery stated in the words of the Apostles' Creed: 'born of the Virgin Mary'. The greatest of them are born of prayer, they are painted with prayer and fasting and thus they become a vehicle for prayer. In fact, when the icons are displayed in museums, onlookers are moved to tears and many bow before the embrace of the holy child who presses his cheek so tenderly against his mother's face that we almost feel his breath upon her flesh. His upturned gaze speaks of mercy and sufferings whose depths are revealed in the dark sorrowing eyes of the mother. He looks at her and she, 'hearing' the mystery of love, looks within, and although his small hands clutch her veil, we know that he is comforter and Lord. Properly understood, these icons are deep spiritual sources.

There is also an ancient tradition of using beads, often just a simple prayer-ring with ten wooden beads and a cross. A friend of mine uses one. She slips it on her finger when she travels by public transport. We will think more about the rosary later, but my friend finds that using these ten beads to pray for people she sees around brings God into the everyday. Traffic jams pass by more quickly when they are used for prayer!

The other day, when we were talking about prayer, two friends who had just come to live in Warsaw said, independently, that as they travel around this foreign city they focus on people's faces and pray for them. I can think of no better way of making yourself feel at home, apart from the great value this prayer is for people who are otherwise unknown. Many people, too, pause when they hear an ambulance rush by and pray for the medical team and the people they are trying to help. All this is part of 'hearing the music of the everyday'.

To return to the Gospels, let us sum up what they tell us about Mary. Mary of Nazareth is a woman whom God chooses. She is a woman who waits and a woman who rejoices. She recognizes her son's authority, but he outgrows her expectations. She is a disciple who doubts, but who is faithful and stands at the cross. She is among the first witnesses of the resurrection. She becomes part of the life of prayer of the Church, and is closely linked with the birthday of the Church, as the following verses from Acts show:

3

And when they had entered, they went up into the upper room where they were staying: Peter, James, John, and Andrew; Philip and Thomas; Bartholomew and Matthew; James the son of Alphaeus and Simon the Zealot; and Judas the son of James. These all continued with one accord in prayer and supplication, with the women and Mary the mother of Jesus, and with his brothers. (Acts 1.13–14)

This is the last time that Mary is named in the New Testament. There is one further reference to the Lord's mother, in Galatians 4.4: 'But when the fullness of the time had come God sent forth his son, born of a woman, born under the Law.'

Mary stands within a great tradition among the mothers of Israel within the old covenant. She traces her lineage directly to David and thus can claim her place in the opening words of that picture of mysterious harmony in Isaiah 11: 'There shall come forth a Rod from the stem of Jesse, and a Branch shall grow out of his roots' (Isaiah 11.1).

These words in turn are woven into an equally mysterious fifteenth-century German Christmas carol: *Es ist ein Ros' entsprungen* – 'a rose has sprung forth from a tender virgin'. And as we read the Gospel story we see that Mary, the young mother-to-be, homeless and seeking a place to rest, is enfolded within the compassion of the one of whom it is written: 'He will feed his flock like a shepherd; he will gather the lambs with his arm, and carry them in his bosom, and gently lead those who are with young' (Isaiah 40.11).

## Miriam of Israel

As we explore the biblical material, I wonder if it would be helpful to use the name 'Miriam' sometimes. This name roots the mother of Yeshua of Nazareth within her language and culture; it is also free of the religious baggage the name 'Mary' has picked up through the Christian centuries.

In the ancient world, and the world of the Bible was no exception, a person's name had great significance. The actual meaning of 'Miriam', however, seems rather obscure. The original Miriam was the sister of Moses, the baby hidden among the reeds and adopted by an Egyptian princess. The young girl's quick wits saved her baby brother (Exodus 1.7). Later in the Old Testament, the prophet Micah mentions Moses' sister in a position of leadership: 'I redeemed you from the house of bondage; and I sent before you Moses, Aaron and Miriam' (Micah 6.4). Miriam of Nazareth, daughter of the covenant, inherits the spiritual legacy of Miriam of the Exodus, the prophet who led the women of Israel in triumphant song:

Then Miriam, the prophetess, the sister of Aaron, took the timbrel in her hand, and all the women went out after her with timbrels and with dances. And Miriam answered them: 'Sing to the LORD, for he has triumphed gloriously! The horse and its rider he has thrown into the sea.' (Exodus 15.20–21)

Miriam seems to have been a popular name in Jesus' day: there are five Marys in the four Gospels. It may be helpful to list them: Mary the mother of Jesus; Mary of Magdala, a town in Galilee; Mary the wife of Cleopas; Mary of

Bethany, sister of Martha and of Lazarus; and Mary the mother of John Mark.

Another Mary is mentioned as the mother of James and Joses. The confusion of names makes it rather unclear, but since these are the names of the Lord's kinsmen I am going to consider this Mary as our Miriam, 'the handmaid of the Lord', whose story starts at home in Nazareth.

When I told this story to children in Russia, I explained that home for Miriam was a simple, one-room house and that the young girl may have been shaking out hand-woven rugs, or shooing out the odd stray chicken, when the angel appeared.

'No, she wasn't,' said Anastasia, a 13-year-old who was in love with half the boys in the class, wove prayer ropes, drew icons and wrote stories which ended up with everyone going off to monasteries. 'Boguroditsa – the God-bearer,' Anastasia continued with conviction, 'was reading the scroll of the book of Isaiah when the angel came.'

This was news to me! 'Tell me more,' I said.

'Boguroditsa was the child of elderly parents called Joachim and Anna. They died when she was three and she was brought up in the temple,' Anastasia informed me with great gusto. Neither of us knew at the time that she, a daughter of Russian Orthodoxy, was quoting the *Proto-evangelium of James*, a very early apocryphal account from second-century Syria which has influenced the way the Eastern Churches understand the nativity. This account says, rather beautifully: 'And Mary was in the temple of the Lord as a dove that is nurtured: and she received food from the hand of an angel.'

The Eastern Orthodox liturgy develops the theme in a complicated interweave of Old Testament events and apocryphal tradition: 'Nourished in faith, O Virgin, with heavenly bread in the Lord's temple, you brought into the world the Bread of Life, the Word of God' (Wybrew, 1997).

And, although I didn't realize it, my more homely picture of a young girl sweeping out a poor room drew on Martin Luther who, anxious to downplay the exalted position of Mary within the medieval church, stressed her insignificance and humility. 'We must believe that she came of poor, despised and lowly parents,' said Luther. 'To her neighbours she was but a simple maiden, tending the cattle and doing the housework' (Wright, 1989).

Life in New Testament times was such that Jewish Miriam would not have been to school. Within Judaism, the 'virtuous woman' had a 'price far above rubies', and although a woman, her husband's helpmeet, could never aspire to an independent role outside the home, the position of Jewish women in the ancient world was far more honourable and secure than that of women in Greek or Roman societies. She was the pivot of the household, the first educator of her sons and daughters, setting their feet on the paths of truth and righteousness – but a young girl would certainly not have studied the Torah, the law, at school with her brothers. 'Let the words of the Torah rather be destroyed by fire than imparted to women,' said the rabbis (Buksbazen, 1963).

## Miriam's world

Miriam of Nazareth, rooted and nurtured within the traditions of the old covenant, would have been taught how to keep her home kosher, how to wash pots correctly and avoid food forbidden in the Old Testament. She could patch worn garments and weave homespun wool. When Jesus says, 'No one sews a piece of unshrunk cloth on an old garment' (Mark 2.21), he must have been thinking of his mother mending his torn clothes in their humble home in Nazareth.

Miriam may have been no older than 12 when we meet her in the pages of Luke's Gospel, but she was already entering adult life, for she was engaged to be married. This meant that she was already legally a wife.

Her husband-to-be, Joseph, was the local joiner. Joseph well deserves further study, and we shall look at him more fully in Chapter 6. The bridal couple lived in Nazareth, a small town where many foreigners – Roman, Greek and Arab – met and mingled with the God-fearing townsfolk. Nazareth lay on a great international highway, from Egypt to Damascus. 'Galilee of the Gentiles', it was called by pure-blooded Judeans in Jerusalem (Matthew 4.15, quoting Isaiah 9.1). 'Can anything good come out of Nazareth?' people asked rhetorically (John 1.46).

But the Gospel story showed that it could – and did!

Galilee was a fertile land, densely populated according to the standards of the day. The first-century Jewish historian Josephus says, 'For the land is everywhere so rich in soil and pasturage and produces such variety of trees that even the most indolent are tempted by these facilities to devote themselves to agriculture' (Buksbazen, 1963).

Galilee, however, had been bled dry by its rapacious rulers. The freedom-loving people of Galilee had forsaken their ploughs for swords in numerous attempts to overthrow the might of Rome.

## God works best when things are worst

The Gospels unfold within political, religious and spiritual turmoil. Jesus' stories show us how the blight of unemployment had hit the peasant farmers of Galilee; religious and civil taxation had impoverished smallholders and traders alike. Yet in these conditions of seeming failure the Messiah was born. This brings us great hope, for it is still in situations of poverty and defeat that the life of God is most richly manifest among people of simple faith. The rule of thumb seems to be that God works best when things are at their worst – because then we trust him most. This is a very hard truth; yet, over again, people find God in the midst of darkness, 'when dove and sun and song are gone'. We are sometimes called to walk through the wilderness and cling to the God we cannot see. When I mentioned this to a friend, she immediately said, 'Oh yes!' She has survived two broken marriages – her first husband abused alcohol and abused her; the second shocked her by divorce after ten years of what she thought was a happy marriage, and then tried to make her responsible for all his debts. Of her five children, one has cut herself off from the family completely: it is thought this young adult has been brainwashed by a sect. Yet this friend of mine has found an inner freedom and daily delights in what the Lord has done for her, taking her through darkness into a life rich in interest, friendships and faith.

For another example of God's grace at work in a dark place, let me return to Poland. At the end of the last century, a great spiritual awakening took place right in the heart of Europe, in communist Poland. Faith took the place of fear, prayer took the place of caution, Christian truth took the place of corruption, hope took the place of drunken despair. If you were looking to find faith in Europe in the closing years of the second millennium, you could find it in Poland. In the days of martial law there was no meat in the shops, but churches were full to over-flowing; there was no bread, but families stood together to say grace. They gave God their tears, their tiredness, their love. Actors and writers, students and housewives, clergy and union men knelt together in puddles and pouring rain to receive the sacrament. The Church became visible in the workplace – and people who longed for change began to find hope.

Similar longings for change lay in the hearts of the oppressed people in Galilee, who lived under the cruel Herodian dynasty, puppet rulers under Rome's control. The Roman general Pompey had invaded Jerusalem some years earlier and desecrated the temple by entering the holy of holies. Things could hardly be worse, but in that darkness, God began to work. The angel came to a young girl in an obscure provincial town.

The Gospel writer Luke names the angel. He is Gabriel. The name means 'God is mighty'. He has already appeared in Scripture in the book of Daniel, where he is described as 'having the appearance of a man' (Daniel 8.15). Daniel falls to the ground prostrate before the heavenly messenger. His narrative continues:

I lifted my eyes and looked, and behold a certain man clothed in linen, whose waist was girded with gold of Uphaz. His body was like beryl, his face like the appear-ance of lightning, his eyes like torches of fire, his arms and feet like burnished bronze in colour, and the sound of his words like the voice of a multitude. (Daniel 10.5–6)

Daniel writes that the men who were with him fled in terror and Daniel himself was left crushed and shaken: 'and no strength remained in me; for my vigour was turned to frailty in me, and I retained no strength' (Daniel 10.8).

## Simple, everyday encounters bring God to earth

The contrast between the Old Testament passage and the story of Miriam of Nazareth couldn't be greater! Here, once again, we see a deep truth of prayer; simple, everyday encounters bring God to earth. This awesome being, before whom Daniel trembled and his servants fled, enters the house in Nazareth. His appearance is not described, but this messenger from God and the young girl speak in a direct and factual dialogue. There is no obscure, high-flown in-jargon, although to begin with he addresses her in high language: 'Rejoice, highly favoured one. The Lord is with you. Blessed are you among women' (Luke 1.28).

It is important to note that Miriam of the Gospels is the recipient – not the dispenser – of God's favour. In sixth-century Syria, a bishop, Jacob of Serug, pointed this out when he wrote:

If there were another, purer and gentler than she, in this one he would dwell, and that one renounce . . . And if there were a soul more splendid and holy, rather than hers, he would choose this one and forsake that one . . . But that the Lord shone from her bodily, his grace it is, may he be praised for so much mercy. (Jacob of Serug, 1995)

11

The young girl, not surprisingly, was 'troubled'. The angel sees her perplexity and reassures her very simply, calling her by name, 'Do not be afraid, Mary.'

We can see from this that God never diminishes our personalities. We may long for the Lord to make enormous changes in us, but in fact God touches us in ways that are most near and dear, so that we find ourselves saying, 'Never have I felt so loved.' Or else, quite simply, 'I felt completely me.'

Our false hopes, our self-regard, our poor feelings about ourselves, our ambitions, our guilt, make us impose conditions of our own making upon the way we imagine God accepts us. And so we let ourselves down all the time – but the amazing truth is that God offers unconditional love. We see this in the encounter between the angel and the girl.

Miriam's priestly kinsman, Zechariah, had been struck dumb when he dared to doubt his God-sent messenger (Luke 1.20). But Miriam freely questions the angel. She has the courage of great simplicity to ask, 'How can this be?' Precisely this focused questioning leads to her unqualified acceptance, 'Let it be to me according to your word'; an affirmation which takes God at his word, no matter what the consequences.

As Miriam questions, the angel patiently explains exactly what will happen. He reminds the young girl that her elderly kinswoman Elizabeth, hitherto barren, is now expecting a child. From this dialogue we learn that we should be totally truthful in prayer. Too often we hide away from our innermost needs. We are scared to face our deepest truths and so we hide from God and dare not ask, 'How can this be?' Let us, like Miriam, learn the courage of simplicity.

Let us note, too, that the angel helps and encourages Miriam, but he does not force her in any way. The choice is hers – and she accepts.

The early Fathers loved to meditate upon Mary's 'let it be'; the whole plan of God's salvation hung upon the young girl's reply. Bernard of Clairvaux describes it like this:

The angel is waiting for your answer: it is time for him to return to God who sent him. We too are waiting . . . for the word of pity, even we who are overwhelmed in wretchedness by the sentence of damnation.

And behold, to you the price of our salvation is offered. If you consent, straightaway shall we be freed . . . by one little word of yours in answer shall we all be made alive . . . Adam asks this of you, O loving Virgin, poor Adam, exiled as he is from paradise with all his poor wretched children; Abraham begs this of you, and David; this all the holy fathers implore, even your fathers, who themselves are dwelling in the valley of the shadow of death; this the whole world is waiting for . . .

Answer, O Virgin, answer the angel speedily; rather, through the angel, answer your Lord. Speak the word, and receive the Word; offer what is yours and conceive what is of God; give what is temporal, and embrace what is eternal . . .

Behold! the Desired of all nations is outside, knocking at your door. Oh! if by your delay he should pass by, and again in sorrow you should have to begin to seek for him whom your soul loves! Arise, then, run and open. Arise by faith, run by the devotion of your heart, open by your word.

13

And Mary said, 'Behold the maidservant of the Lord. Let it be to me according to your word' (Luke 1.38). (Kenneth, 1983)

Miriam responded intelligently to the angel. She trusted God and let the Lord invade her deepest self in a physical way that has never been asked of anyone else, before or since. She is unique because she bore the Son of God in her body, and brought him to birth. Her 'let it be' is both willing, active assent and humble submission. In this she is a true daughter of the covenant. She agrees to walk the way through the wilderness, although her betrothal promises to Joseph will now be called into question, and her honour, and even her life itself, are under threat. She has been offered Presence – with a real threat of being cast out, even annihilated. Sometimes we too are called to find Presence when all we can sense is absence: the absence of God, the absence of hope. There seems no way through the crushing darkness. God says to the people of Israel, 'I bore you on eagle's wings and brought you to myself' (Exodus 19.4). The picture is of a mother eagle teaching her young to fly. But when we are in the wilderness, the beating wings of the great golden eagle seem to carry others, but there seems no place there for us. Or else we neither see nor hear them, so great seems the darkness.

But the Bible assures us that the wings are there, that they are always there for you and for me, that the mother eagle who 'stirs up the nest' to tilt the young out into the cold, thin air is hovering beneath her frightened chicks, and her wings are outstretched to swoop down and carry her young. 'As an eagle stirs up its nest, hovers over its young, spreading out its wings, taking them up, carrying them on its wings, so the LORD alone led him, and there was no foreign god with him' (Deuteronomy 32.11–12).

The Bible promises us that there is light in the darkness. Isaiah's tremendous promise echoes with unabated power across multi-millennia: 'The people who walked in darkness have seen a great light; those who dwell in the land of the shadow of death, upon them a light has shined' (Isaiah 9.2). Please note: it is the people who walk in darkness who see the light. But perhaps you, like me, cry out, 'Yes, yes, I believe the light is there, but I can't see it. I believe the overshadowing wings are there, but I can't feel them.'

And, as for flying, no! We are grounded, hopelessly so. Then let's be kind to ourselves within the darkness. At one point I asked a friend, 'How do I cope?' And she replied, 'Try to make your niche as comfortable as possible.'

It is the best advice I have ever received! Stop striving for what isn't and try to make what is as bearable as possible. Some people join a gym, others go out running or cycling or climb mountains. For myself, I have a bath. A bath for me is far more than just getting clean: it's a retreat. Of course, you can't do that with small children clamouring to get into the bubbles too. But we can all find our own way to create that necessary niche for ourselves within the darkness and make it as comfortable as we can.

This is not escapism. It is a way of enabling us to say, 'Let it be!' It helps us go deeper into the words of the prophet Zephaniah, which we applied to Mary in the Prologue: 'I will leave in your midst a meek and humble people, and they shall trust in the name of the LORD' (Zephaniah 3.12). But this is never one-sided. The prophecy continues, 'He will rejoice over you with gladness, he will quiet you in his love' (Zephaniah 3.17).

15

Therefore we trust, therefore we love. And, says Julian of Norwich, 'Love maketh might and wisdom full meek to us' (Julian of Norwich, 1961). Love encountered Miriam of Nazareth with might and wisdom when the angel, the messenger of the Lord, entered her home and answered her questions most meekly. Love made might and wisdom full meek within her womb.

## 'Then the angel left her'

Perhaps some of the most poignant words in the Bible are Luke's: 'Then the angel left her.' Miriam is left alone with the consequences of her 'yes'. Nothing will ever be the same again. She must take her secret glory out into the world, where the pressures of life will threaten to quench her inner fire, where misunderstandings will arise and fears will beset her, and doubts will drown out that first great hope with their insistent clamour.

Miriam must have been caught between fear and joy; afraid of the changes within her, even while she welcomed them; afraid of what others would say. Especially Joseph, to whom she was betrothed. She could hold her head high among gossips, but his opinion of her, his bride-to-be, counted for everything.

She needed someone to talk to, someone who would understand. But to whom could she turn? Not to her mother! It is hard enough for a young girl to tell her mother, 'I'm pregnant'. Far worse, how could this young girl say, 'I carry the hope of Israel within me. God has begotten my unborn child.' In her need and loneliness Miriam went to stay with the only person who could help her, the person the angel had mentioned. She went to stay with her cousin Elizabeth.

As we imagine Miriam's hopes and fears, we may reflect that God also comes to us, humbly, as he came to her. God touched the young girl in her humanity, in her femininity, and he touches us, too, in deeply personal ways. We may be afraid, but if, like Miriam, we accept what God is doing in our lives, he will not leave us without someone to comfort us. Like Miriam, we shall find our Elizabeth, a person who knows and understands. Then, like Miriam, we will be prepared to undertake a journey of affirmation and delight in the ways of God.

## To ponder

Hearing the music of the everyday and turning it into prayer helps us find sustenance when 'dove and sun' seem to be gone. Meditate on the picture of God the mother eagle, who tips up the nest so that the chicks must stretch their wings and fly, but who is always hovering close by, ready to carry her young on her outspread wings.

We use the words of the Christian creeds, 'born of the Virgin Mary' or 'was incarnate from the Holy Spirit and the Virgin Mary'. Echoing the Gospel greeting of the angel, a very old prayer from the Coptic Church draws out the mystery contained within these statements of belief:

Hail Mary, the most beautiful dove, which carried the Word of God for us; we greet you with the Archangel Gabriel, saying: hail, full of grace, the Lord is with you! Hail, O Virgin, glory of our race, you have carried Emmanuel for us. We pray that you will remember us before our Lord Jesus Christ, that he will forgive our sins. (Day, 1972)

17

# CHAPTER 2

# *Journeying with a secret joy*

———•———

Miriam of Nazareth accepted the favour and blessing of the God of Israel. And, having given her consent to the Lord, she took immediate action. This seems to be a trend all through the Bible. God calls, and nothing is quite the same again. But he does not leave us unsupported. The classic example is Saul of Tarsus. Blinded and over-whelmed by his encounter with the risen Lord Jesus, Saul is led into Damascus, but God provides a counsellor, who greets him with love and speaks a word of power which heals Saul so that he is filled with the Holy Spirit (Acts 9.3, 8, 10–18).

We can learn from Mary of Nazareth how to respond positively and appropriately to the call of God. The young girl takes note of the words spoken by the angel about her cousin Elizabeth. Realizing that here is someone who will listen and, she hopes, understand, she sets out at once to see her. She doesn't delay. I think this is important. If we feel God call, and do not take action, the gentle flame of the Spirit will flicker and soon be extinguished, for God never forces us. Miriam's example shows us how important it is to seek prayerful contact with the person who is most likely to help us.

In her walk with God, Miriam shares something of the path taken by the great-grandmother of King David. Ruth the Moabite woman chose the stigma of childless widow-hood and poverty rather than desert her mother-in-law Naomi. The action of the book of Ruth is set in Bethlehem. Ruth, following the precepts of the Law, gleans in the fields and seeks the protection of her dead father-in-law's relative, Boaz, who marries the homeless woman. The book ends with joy, but to attain this joy Ruth had to make a step of commitment and trust, heedless of the outcome: 'Ruth said, "Entreat me not to leave you, or to turn back from following after you . . . Your people shall be my people, and your God, my God"' (Ruth 1.16).

Miriam, too, has made her commitment and now she sets out on a journey, travelling with trepidation and with secret joy. Luke sketches the story in a few words. I like the immediacy of the Good News version: 'Mary got ready and hurried off to a town in the hill country of Judea. She went into Zechariah's house and greeted Elizabeth' (Luke 1.39–40, GNB).

During her journey, bumpy and tiring as it was, Miriam's thoughts would have been full of her amazing encounter with the angel. She was radiant with the knowledge that God had blessed her in such a special way, and, like every young mother, she longed to hold her baby in her arms. What would he be like, she must have wondered, this child of the Most High? But there must have been many hard questions troubling her too, and fear. She was glad to be escaping from prying eyes to the seclusion of her cousin's home.

## Journeying with a secret joy

We are not told how Miriam travelled to her kinswoman,

19

nor how long the journey took – it was a distance of about 120 kilometres from Nazareth to Jerusalem. We may imagine a three or four day journey, in the company of other travellers, merchants maybe. We, too, are often called to make a journey towards God. Let us take Miriam of Nazareth as a guide. Sometimes our journey may be an actual, physical movement away from home and the everyday: a pilgrimage, retreat, house-party, where we draw aside, trusting that God will meet us or speak to us. We can also make a symbolic, inner journey, alone or with a trusted friend. Or we can cut loose and wander, something done by backpackers everywhere. If we do this, we have to realize that the world is a dangerous place for people who travel alone, and we also have to be careful not to use our spiritual journey as a pretext to sponge off others.

However, cutting loose for God is an ancient Christian custom – the early Irish missionary monks called their journey into the unknown 'the white martyrdom'. It's a Russian tradition too. A painting in the Russian Museum in St Petersburg called 'The Hermit' depicts an old man with flowing white hair and beard among the lakes and forests of pre-revolutionary Russia. The transparency of his spirit is highlighted by the way the blue, green and gold of the autumnal landscape shines through his threadbare, crumpled robes. I bought a postcard of the painting – and later that day met an elderly man with flowing white locks. He was an exact counterpart, except he wore a suit of ancient tweed and was Danish, not Russian, but he was a hermit monk, just the same, making his own journey from affluence and comfort towards God.

Even in the years before the collapse of communism in the former Soviet Union, Russian people travelled great distances to seek spiritual counsel from hermit monks, the 'startsy' or elders who have made themselves so paper-thin on earth that the reality of heaven shines almost visibly through them. Possessed with spiritual gifts which could never be explained in material terms, they officially didn't exist in state-controlled religious life.

One such elder was called Tavrion. Born in 1898, he ran away from home when he was 13, but not to see the world or make his fame and fortune. The young Russian boy ran away to God and became a monk. When he was 30 years old he was arrested and spent the next 27 years in labour camp or exile. Set free in 1956, Tavrion later spoke of those years of privation and imprisonment with joy.

## Keeping the balance between the external life of labour and the inner life of the heart

The vast forests of Russia have been hallowed by its saints. They sought refuge there from the world and toiled with their own hands to wrest food from the soil, only to find that serfs and princes, countesses and peasant women sought them out in their seclusion for prayer and advice. It has been said that the great contribution of the desert fathers was their emphasis on the balance between the external life of labour and the inner life of the heart – and it was this important balance which Russian spirituality has inherited.

It is a balance which Miriam of Nazareth found when she went about her daily life in Nazareth and 'kept all these things, and pondered them in her heart' (Luke 2.19, AV). This balance of contemplation and action is lacking in twenty-first-century consumer society, where those who have no paid employment feel devalued, while those who are salaried are driven and have no time. Miriam's hidden life, together with her readiness to undertake great things for God, show us how this balance can be maintained. Part of it has to do with 'hearing the music of the everyday', which we considered in the last chapter.

Tavrion found enforced toil in the forests a privilege and a blessing. Even though he was a prisoner, he laboured and prayed as the saints had done; a regular rhythm of life which drew him closer to God. Finally, he was invited to a monastery in Riga in Latvia. Before long, crowds flocked to him. Tavrion knew their needs – his prayers brought healing, his knowledge and discernment enabled people to put their lives to rights and to begin to live in conformity with God in a totally atheist state.

He died in 1978. Russia was still firmly held in the stranglehold of official atheism; but the life and fire of the Holy Spirit will always draw people, and hundreds of people from every layer of Soviet society flocked to Tavrion – as Miriam, too, was drawn to Elizabeth.

## The meeting of two mothers-to-be

Elizabeth, Simeon and Anna (whom we shall meet in Chapter 4) were all hidden people, and perhaps none more so than Elizabeth in these last months of her late and unexpected pregnancy. Long past the first flush of youth, she may well have been the butt of gossip, a kind of nine months' wonder. I imagine Elizabeth sheltering at home, hiding from prying eyes. We may picture her pushing back her greying hair and turning her burdened body wearily when, one glad day, light footsteps run to her curtained threshold and a young voice calls her name.

The joyful meeting of these two pregnant women is one of the most moving and significant encounters in Scripture. Their encounter throbs with prophetic vision and with messianic hope. There is a lovely moment in Jacob of Serug's poem from sixth-century Syria in which Elizabeth bends her swollen body towards her young kinswoman, Mary, and shows her the exact words in the scroll where it is written that Emmanuel, the servant of God, will be born of a young woman (Isaiah 7.14).

> For three months the sublime and divine story was being told in the house of the priest on account of Mary... Then while the old woman was meditating on Isaiah and reading, she explained and showed to Mary all which had been said: 'Behold, my daughter, in the prophecy it is written that the virgin will conceive... Take with you also that scroll of the prophecy and give it to your betrothed to read all of it and to understand it.' (Jacob of Serug, 1995)

We can enjoy this picture of the older woman expounding Scripture to her young cousin, no matter how we understand the word translated as 'virgin' in older versions and 'young woman' in more modern ones.

The keynote of Elizabeth's joy and Miriam's response is faith, pure and simple. At the sound of Miriam's greeting, Elizabeth's unborn baby, who will 'go ahead of the Lord to prepare his road for him', leaps for joy within his mother's womb. Elizabeth, filled with the Holy Spirit, blesses Miriam with the authority and fervour of an anointed prophet:

'Blessed are you among women and blessed is the fruit of your womb' (Luke 1.42).

Let us pause to meditate on these words. No one, not even Miriam herself, has told Elizabeth that her young kinswoman is pregnant. There could, of course, have been no hasty telephone calls, no e-mails. But Miriam does not need to speak. The Holy Spirit has overshadowed her. She is flooded with holy, secret joy, the hidden life of the Son of God within her.

Amazingly, we too carry the life of Christ in us. 'God's plan is to make known his secret to his people, this rich and glorious secret which he has for all peoples,' writes Paul (Colossians 1.27, GNB). And what is this secret? Staggeringly enough it is this: 'Christ in you, the hope of glory.'

Yes, we carry the Christ-life within us! Yet so much within us seems to resist its growth. I find it particularly helpful, therefore, to reflect upon this meeting of two mothers-to-be; so joyful, so simple, so overflowing with faith and delight, so truly pregnant with spiritual truth, so potent, that its finale is Miriam's Magnificat, a 'pearl of great price' among the great statements in Scripture about God and his covenant mercy.

## Hospitality and mutual delight

Secluded, possibly more than a little frightened of the trauma of birth, Elizabeth must have felt very lonely. Her husband can no longer speak and Elizabeth is carrying his frustration and chastisement too. But now God visits her in the most tender, most acceptable way possible: through her young kinswoman. If Miriam needed

Elizabeth's counsel and advice, Elizabeth needed Miriam's companionship and trust. She unreservedly accepts the young girl and her unborn child. Jacob of Serug compares the two women to the morning and evening, dawn and dusk. He writes:

> The maiden and the old woman granted me a tale full of wonder; love moves me, that while I am marvelling I may speak of it . . . The old woman is similar to evening which enshrouds and buries the light in its old age. The maiden is similar to the east, the mother of the early morning which carries the day in its bosom to bring it to earth. Morning and evening look at each other lovingly, so that in youth and old age a sense of wonder may increase. Morning which carries the great Sun of Righteousness, and evening in which is the star that proclaims concerning the Light. (Jacob of Serug, 1995)

Elizabeth, the older, married woman, the priest's wife, a person of status, mysteriously touched by God, reverences the unwed girl. 'Why is this granted to me, that the mother of my Lord should come to me?' cries Elizabeth (Luke 1.43). This affirmation unabashedly acknowledges Miriam's role as 'the mother of my Lord' – a clear statement that Jesus, the child to be born of her, is none other than the Holy One of God, Christ the Lord. How that acceptance must have heartened Miriam! She must have felt cherished, ready to face whatever lay ahead of her, no matter how much pain she would have to bear, no matter the personal cost to her. It sometimes takes a lot of faith and love to acknowledge the hidden potential in one another, and this can be particularly true across the generation gap.

Elizabeth has given Miriam full and free hospitality. She has offered her young cousin a place in which both women can share their mutual delight in Miriam's motherhood, and, doubtless, in Elizabeth's pregnancy too. Out of this loving acceptance comes Miriam's great, prophetic song.

## The art and discipline of blessing

There is great power in blessing, particularly in our home and family life. Criticism is destructive and inhibiting. Blessing, approval and praise make children and adults grow. In Judaism, it seems there are blessings for everything. A friend who had given up on belief told me that he now had a big problem: what to do about the blessings? So on Yom Kippur he made a pilgrimage to the river bank, where he smoked a cigarette and quietly watched the water flow by, a sad honouring of a holy day. The writer Marge Piercy shows how blessings can be woven into everyday life. Her book of poems, *The Art of Blessing the Day*, is an affirmation of the music of the everyday. She shows us that blessing is an art, and like every art it requires discipline, as the title poem explains:

> . . . the discipline of blessings is to taste
> each moment, the bitter, the sour, the sweet
> and the salty, and be glad for what does not
> hurt. The art is compressing attention
> to each little and big blossom of the tree
> of life, to let the tongue sing each fruit,

its savor, its aroma and its use . . . Bless whatever you can
with eyes and hands and tongue. If you
can't bless it, get ready to make it new.

(Piercy, 1998)

In the encounter between the two mothers-to-be,
Elizabeth uses the word 'blessed' three times. It has been
said that when a word or phrase is repeated not twice
but three times in Scripture, then this is a sure indication
that we should take special note of it. Let us practise the
art of blessing, for when we bless one another we grow in
love; out of this comes the praise of the Lord.

## My soul, my spirit rejoice in my Saviour . . .

The Magnificat stands within the prophetic tradition of
the Old Testament. The earliest woman singer was, we
have seen, Miriam, who led the women in a triumphant
shout of praise which echoes in the opening words of the
Magnificat. Another great mother of Israel was the prophet
Deborah. Her war-like shout of praise is thought to be
one of the earliest poems in the Bible. It goes beyond the
purely personal. Unlike the Magnificat, it is addressed to
the leaders of the land. 'Hear, O kings! Give ear, O princes'
(Judges 5.3).

Gloriously blood-curdling, true 'Braveheart' stuff, this
song of a powerful woman is concerned for justice and
for the poor, just as is Mary's Magnificat. Deborah heaps
scorn on the tribes who don't turn out to fight: 'Why did
you sit among the sheepfolds, to hear the pipings for the
flocks?' (Judges 5.16). She praises an act of murder when

27

the much-feared leader, Sisera, with 900 chariots of iron, is tricked and killed by a woman, Jael:

> Most blessed among women is Jael ... blessed is she among women in tents. He asked for water, she gave milk; she brought out cream in a lordly bowl. She stretched out her hand to the tent peg. Her right hand to the workmen's hammer. She pounded Sisera ... At her feet he sank, he fell, where he sank, there he fell dead. (Judges 5.24–27)

Her last verse opens up the area of God's covenant love which the Magnificat develops: 'let those who love Him be like the sun when it comes out in full strength' (Judges 5.31). Deborah understands that strength depends on commitment to God. Miriam sees that it leads to spiritual victory: 'He has shown strength with his arm. He has scattered the proud in the imagination of their hearts' (Luke 1.51). Deborah affirms God's righteousness; Miriam of Nazareth praises his mercy. The words 'most blessed among women' which describe Jael are applied by Miriam to herself. But Mary of Nazareth knows that she is called blessed because of what God has done for her: 'For he who is mighty has done great things for me' (Luke 1.49).

The strong praise-poem by a strong woman sets Miriam of Nazareth in a great tradition. Deborah is unafraid to affirm, 'I, even I will sing to the LORD; I will sing praise to the LORD God of Israel.' She clearly needs no assertiveness training! In this she is unlike Hannah, a woman whose song is closer to Mary's. Like Elizabeth, Hannah had borne the stigma of childlessness for many years. She takes her sorrow to the Lord, receives her heart's desire and praises God in prophetic words which link her personal joy to the position of the poor and downtrodden: 'The LORD makes poor and makes rich. He brings low and lifts up. He raises the poor from the dust and lifts the beggar from the ash heap, to set them among princes and make them inherit the throne of glory' (1 Samuel 2.7–8). Hannah's praise more closely anticipates Miriam's and shows a more developed concept of God's fatherly love than Deborah's wilder song.

## He who is mighty has done great things for me

Deborah the prophet-mother in Israel and Hannah the mother whose child was dedicated to the Lord both antic-ipate Mary, who stands on the boundary between the old covenant and the new. Miriam is a daughter of Israel who is directly descended from the sweet singer of the Lord, the shepherd-king David. Her song echoes the great praises of the psalms, both in structure and content. She revels in the greatness of God and is unafraid to declare: 'henceforth all generations will call me blessed'. This strong prophetic statement will be fulfilled in Luke 11.27 when a woman declares to Jesus, 'Blessed is the womb that bore you and the breasts which nursed you.' But Jesus replies, 'Blessed are those who hear the word of God and keep it' (Luke 11.28). Some have seen this as judgement on Miriam, a way of negating her and affirming the new family of faith instead. However, Miriam, a daughter of the Old Testament, is a disciple within the New. The family may have doubted (we shall discuss this later) but Miriam has heard and obeyed the word of God. She deserves to be called 'blessed' in the positive sense which Jesus means.

## Holy is his name – this life-changing prayer

Miriam's 'holy is his name' (Luke 1.49) takes our thoughts forward to her son's great family prayer which unites Christians of all traditions: 'Our Father in heaven, hallowed be your name . . .' (Matthew 6.9). Once again, we see that Mary of Nazareth links the faith-world of the Old Testament with that of the New.

Evelyn Underhill, a writer on prayer, reminds us that these four words, 'hallowed (or holy) be your name', are not only the essence of religion; they actually reshape the whole of our personal life. Our entire focus changes. No longer is our aim what we want: a bigger house, a new car or a holiday in an exotic part of the world. Instead, we submit our plans to the holy name. When we do so we join our praise to the whole of creation. 'Let everything that has breath praise the Lord,' says the very last prayer in the book of Psalms (150.6).

'Holy is his name.' We pay lip-service to these words, but dare we really utter this life-changing prayer? Let us reflect that Miriam takes no holiness or glory to herself. She rejoices in God and on the good things he has done for her and for his people.

For if there is power in blessing and affirming one another, as we have seen in the meeting of Mary and Elizabeth, how much more power is there in blessing and affirming the name of the Lord! History shows us that thousands have died with the holy name on their lips, turning their murder into an act of testimony which made them not passive victims of crimes beyond all enormity, but people witnessing to a God beyond all understanding. This was true, too, in the slave labour camps of the Soviet Union. The system aimed to degrade and dehumanize, but the blessing and love of prisoners cracked the iron curtain. Prayer and active involvement on their behalf all over the world also lit candles in the darkness. These flames of love flared into light – and this should not be forgotten as we move into a new era.

It is worth recalling that in Nazi Germany a group of deeply Christian men, including Helmut von Moltke, a young father of two small children, and a diplomat, Hans Berndt von Haeften, 14 years married and father of five, made a stand against tyranny. They were incriminated in a plot to assassinate Hitler and hanged. What is little known is the fate and faith of their wives. Barbara von Haeften, breastfeeding her two-month-old baby, was arrested and learnt of her husband's execution while she herself was in prison. In her cell, a widow, newly bereaved and not knowing what would happen to her or the children, this remarkable woman maintained a life of prayer, gaining comfort from the New Testament and the hymn book. (The pastor who visited her explained that the authorities did not permit the Old Testament – it was a Jewish book.) Before every meal she prayed the Lord's Prayer. She found that the words 'Your will be done' stuck in her throat . . . yet she kept on praying without self-pity or complaint.

## He has filled the hungry . . . and sent the rich away empty

Miriam of Nazareth voices the longings of the despised

and downcast among her people. Her song looks forward to the heart of the gospel, the 'Good News of Jesus Christ, the Son of God' (Mark 1.1, GNB). She empowers the humblest believer to stand straight and affirm our dignity as a child of the Father. Like Hannah, her thoughts go out from her personal joy to the poor of Israel. She prophesies a revolution, not of force but of love: the hungry will be fed while the rich go away empty; the mighty shall be put down, the humble lifted high. Two thousand years later we are no nearer to understanding what all this really means, or living it out in our lives.

Mary's Magnificat anticipates the Beatitudes. For Jesus will develop this truth in the sermon on the mount: blessed are the humble, the despised, the empty, the broken-hearted . . . (Matthew 5.3–10).

We have seen that the Jewish mother was the first instructor of her children. We may well imagine Miriam, busy about her household tasks in Nazareth, telling her first-born son about the day the angel came, about the great promise of salvation, about her song of praise. Mother Miriam would undoubtedly have instructed Yeshua in the tradition of his people. Jesus may well have learnt from his mother the great paradox of power made perfect in weakness. He will encapsulate that teaching in the timeless story of the religious leader who came to God with his piety and self-righteousness and went away empty, while the sinful tax collector went away filled (Luke 18.9–14).

## The revelation of the glory

Bach's music captures the essence of this paradox with a musical joke. In his setting of the Magnificat the rich are

sent away without any music – the phrase ends on a rest!
Let us listen to this silence. It is the heart of the gospel. A
friend of mine, after a lifetime given to prayer, has called
this the 'mystery of mysteries', before which words fail. He
has written,

> I keep returning to the deepest affirmation of St John's
> Gospel: the Passion is the revelation of the Glory – not
> something that has to be gone through in order to get
> at a subsequent glory, it is the Glory of Love to share, to
> take on, get inside the pain of others.

Miriam, the young unmarried girl in Nazareth, is called
into the heart of the mystery. And she rejoices in the Lord.

Here we have not liberation theology, but the theology
of inner liberation. It's not something we're at ease with,
especially because we live in a society which frantically
tries to extend and enrich the life of the rich, even to the
point of human cloning and the creation of 'designer
babies'. We are scared of missing out, we are scared of
defect; we are scared, above all, of death.

It is hard to resist technology which promises well-
being, not least because we shrink from the grossly handi-
capped, the bizarrely mentally sick, the abusive problem
family. Our society is kinder to our pets, which cannot
think or love, than to the mentally and physically impaired,
who can do both, even if it is slowly. Miriam would not
have understood our attitude. Her song shows us how
wrong we are. As we heard in the Prologue,

> mast and plough are made
> from this felled and damaged tree
> whose canticle awoke the sun.

Just as it is 'the people who walk in darkness' who see the light, so too it is the lame who will leap for joy.

## Miriam's prayer glorifies God – and gloats in his approval

Miriam's song also shows us a pattern of prayer which glorifies God and is self-forgetful. Too often we anxiously submit our plans to God as if we were employees asking the managing director for his rubber stamp of approval. But Miriam gloats in God! I think there will always be a tension in prayer between asking for what we want and letting that go and truly delighting in the Lord. There is a danger that the first kind of prayer will either leave us with a sense of self-importance or only increase our anxieties and fears. And what we long for is that our hungry hearts should be filled to overflowing with God. Miriam's Magnificat sets the pattern and shows the way.

She sees God's mercy as extending 'from generation to generation . . . for ever.' Miriam of Nazareth bears witness to the importance of our spiritual ancestry. 'We are surrounded by such a great cloud of witnesses', says Hebrews 12.1. Miriam understands that salvation is for here and now but that it also stretches beyond us. Her song of praise carries us into a dimension we can never fully understand. But we discover it when we welcome one another, as Elizabeth welcomed her young cousin, delighting in what unites us, blessing each other and enjoying the differences which make each of us unique.

## To ponder

This rich and glorious secret: Christ in you, the hope of glory. We birth Christ in the fullness of his risen life within ourselves and within one another when we bless the Lord and affirm each other. Practise the discipline of blessing – and be joyful!

CHAPTER 3

# The heart of love

---•---

## Stars and angels, dust and dung as well as doves

Mary of Nazareth is a daughter of the covenant. Her spiritual ancestry is expressed in her Magnificat, which ends: 'He has helped his servant Israel in remembrance of his mercy, as he spoke to our fathers, to Abraham and his seed for ever' (Luke 1.54–55).

The story of the covenant stretches far, far back in time, to the glory and freshness of Eden, when perfect innocence was tempted by imperfect knowledge. The worm entered the apple, the sweet fruit soured and darkness fell. But we know that love and protection continually surrounded the people of the covenant. 'I bore you on eagles' wings and brought you to myself,' says the Lord (Exodus 19.4). We saw that the picture is reinforced with astonishing force and tenderness in the book of Deuteronomy: 'As an eagle stirs up its nest, hovers over its young, spreading out its wings, taking them up, carrying them on its wings, so the LORD alone led him [Israel]' (Deuteronomy 32.11).

This is the love song of the Bible. If we trust this nurturing eagle we will leave the nest of our fears and insecurities and allow ourselves to be carried above the highest crags. We, too, shall learn to fly. Miriam of Nazareth shows us what it means to be enfolded by the encircling wings of a golden eagle who soars within the eddies of the winds above the mountain heights. Miriam trusted God completely. She let herself be carried, let herself soar – and became the means by which God brought redemption into the world.

'Daughter of poor ones, who became mother of the Lord of Kings and gave riches to a needy world that it might live from him,' sang Jacob of Serug, the Syrian songwriter. Let us stay with these words. For one of the ways in which the needy world 'lives from' the birth of the Lord into a human family is that every new family now becomes the holy family, no matter what stresses and disappointments later occur. We learn that God is present in our greatest joy as well as our greatest need, and this is especially true in our family lives. As we absorb these words, holding our family lives within the light of the holy family, we glimpse a new depth to the meaning of 'mercy'.

Miriam must have made the bed of hay as comfortable as she could for her baby – but hay prickles. Later, curling wood shavings from the carpenter's bench between her fingers, Miriam may have been reminded of the cattle shed.

> I curl
> fragile tissue, soft as hay
> between my fingers . . .

Our relationships, especially in our homes and families, often need special nurture, special tenderness. They can be fragile, soft, yet full of prickles. In the library of books which make the Bible, the Song of Solomon, celebrating physical love, contains a warning about relationships: 'Catch us the foxes, the little foxes that spoil the vines, for our vines have tender grapes' (Song of Solomon 2.15). Within the vineyards and gardens of our relationships, let us watch out for those 'little foxes' with their snapping jaws. They prey upon sweetness and ruin trust. As we follow the Lord's mother through her family life we will see how she had to contend with snapping foxes in many different shapes and sizes. Criticism is one of the worst, for us as it was for Miriam. Putting one another down in front of others is another nasty little fox. Deceit, lying, infidelity are obvious ones. Taking each other for granted is yet another – and so the list can go on.

The 'mother of the Lord of Kings', who had nowhere to lay her newborn child, shows us how the love of the heavenly Father permeates our homes and our relationships. In deeper ways than we can imagine, the Father-heart of the Lord understands how fragile we can be. And because God was born and nurtured within a human family, we too may feel encouraged to work at the vexed and often vexing issues in our family lives. For this is what the incarnation means: our effort and achievement, our joys and our brokenness and hurt are woven into a deep unity with the creator of all. What can be more frail than a newborn baby – and yet what unfathomable potential is stored within that tiny form?

Over the years, as I've prayed for my family and the families of friends, the prayers of Scripture have become a real lifeline, and particularly those of the apostle Paul in Ephesians. Here is one of them in full:

For this reason I fall on my knees before the Father, from whom every family in heaven and on earth receives its true name. I ask God from the wealth of his glory to give you power through his Spirit to be strong in your inner selves, and I pray that Christ will make his home in your hearts through faith. I pray that you may have your roots and foundation in love, so that you, together with all God's people, may have the power to understand how broad and long, how high and deep, is Christ's love. Yes, may you come to know his love – although it can never be fully known – and so be completely filled with the very nature of God.

To him who by means of his power working in us is able to do so much more than we can ever ask for, or even think of: to God be glory in the church and in Christ Jesus for all time, for ever and ever! Amen. (Ephesians 3.14–20, GNB)

I sometimes find it helpful to select a couple of verses, particularly verses 16–18, and substitute the name of the family member for whom I pray, followed by 'he' or 'she' in place of the pronoun 'you'. As well as using this prayer for established families, we could also offer it for and to our friends who are about to embark on marriage and, they hope, on family life.

And when marriages break down and families are sundered and hurt, Paul's prayer assures us that God's 'power working in us is able to do so much more than we can ever ask for, or even think of'. Let us weave these words into prayer for those we love most. Unfortunately, when relationships cause us distress we often feel like cutting loose. We know we should try to restore the broken harmony, to weave together frayed threads of misunderstanding, but the task is so hard that we often don't know how to begin. Some things can be changed or negotiated. Others can't, and then the pain is too great to be borne.

Yet we glimpse the holy family in the cattle shed, surrounded by stars and angels, yes, but by dust and dung as well as doves. Can this lead us into the kind of prayer we mentioned in the Prologue, that lets things be as they are? I am in no way suggesting that anyone should stay in an abusive relationship. The simple faith that says 'let it be' adds, 'according to your word'. But the birth of Christ as a human child shows us that the Word has been made little. Little enough for us to acknowledge our frailty, and to pray, just one word: 'Abba', perhaps, or 'love', or even, simply, 'help'! That short prayer-word may be the seed which grows into the tree of life which will bring healing to us and those we love. Birthing her child was only the beginning for Miriam of Nazareth. She would have to grow with him and learn her need of help and healing from the cattle shed to the cross.

## 'The earth gives a cave to the unapproachable'

Some traditions say that Jesus was born not in a stable but in a cave in the hills. The origin of this is the same nativity account from second-century Syria which young Anastasia was unwittingly quoting in St Petersburg when she told me that Boguroditsa had been brought up in the temple. This Syrian manuscript says that Jesus was born in this way: a great light shone within a cave and when it faded the newborn child was revealed. The Eastern

Orthodox liturgy weaves the tradition into a prayer which celebrates the transcendent creator God who makes himself one with his creatures: 'The Virgin today gives birth to him who is above being . . . The earth gives a cave to the unapproachable' (Wybrew, 1997).

The early accounts also state that Joseph was an old man when he was betrothed to Mary. This is because Mary is assumed to remain a virgin after the birth, as well as beforehand, and indeed great treatises were written to show that she actually remained a virgin during childbirth. Nativity icons of the Eastern Orthodox Church always show Joseph as elderly. Mary is called 'ever-virgin'. The understanding of sexuality which made virginity greater than matrimony is very foreign to our modern frame of reference. It has actually put the virginity of Mary on a pedestal and made it more important than her humble faith and total trust.

The Gospels certainly tells us that Mary was unmarried when she conceived the child who was to save all people, and we shall think this through as we follow the holy family through Chapters 5 and 6 and when we examine the question of the Lord's brothers in Chapter 7. But for now let's set the issue of virginity aside and contemplate the cave, for there is a symbol here which takes us to the language of myth and dream. Many mythic journeys take the wanderer into the underground through caverns with openings so small that the traveller must stoop and crawl into the dark. In many myths, too, the cave is the womb where new life begins, and since the pilgrim must stoop and the opening is small, the pilgrim must make herself, himself very small. Jesus consented to make that journey. He taught by word and example that the way to the new birth in the Spirit is to listen for the wind of the Spirit which blows where it wills; and then to be compliant enough to turn and face its direction. In the Prologue Miriam sings:

> of poppies in scarlet dress,
> bending as the wind directs;
> of sickles scything pliant corn;
> of wine and oil:
> seepings of vat and press.

The dance of the poppies and the harvest of corn, oil and wine are images of the secret work of the Spirit: of the willingness of the disciple to hear and bend like poppies, like corn; even to be crushed, like grapes, like olives so that the Father may work his will.

And the way to do this is to become little (as Jesus asked us to be). Then we may hear him say, 'Do not fear, little flock, for it is your Father's good pleasure to give you the kingdom' (Luke 12.32). The gentle concept of the 'little flock' is reminiscent of the picture in Zephaniah of the 'meek and humble people' over whom the Lord rejoices. We understand that Jesus' kingdom teaching was rooted in the prophets of the Old Testament, the covenant Miriam sees fulfilled in the birth of her child. The teaching takes us back to Isaiah: the Saviour of Israel, whose triumph is announced from the mountain tops, comes with power and strength, yet 'will feed his flock like a shepherd; he will gather the lambs within his arm, and carry them in his bosom, and gently lead those that are with young' (Isaiah 40.11). It takes us to Miriam of Nazareth. God, writes Jacob of Serug, looked on Miriam's humility and gentleness 'and dwelt in her because it is easy for him to dwell with the humble'.

When we contemplate the newborn baby and the humility and gentleness of the mother we learn a new dimension, one which it is impossible to put into words, but which we may be able to turn into prayer. The lesson of such helpless humility is that we are flung into the heart of God's love.

## Christ comes to us in kindness

The picture of poppies also conjures up a landscape of joy. Commercial development, motorways and vast farms have swallowed up the countryside, but poppies and other wild flowers still bless waste ground with beauty. They sing of grace: no one has planted them. No one looks after them. They just are.

Flowers in all cultures have a very deep meaning. Visitors to Poland, for example, are amazed at the riot of flowers on sale. Flowers are presented at birthdays and saints' name-days or whenever you go visiting. At weddings the bride is overwhelmed by them! In Russia, people from the audience come forward after every concert with flowers for their favourite performers. Russians who attend concerts else-where are quite shocked when this doesn't happen. However, their enduring memory of the UK is neat front gardens, bright with flowers. People the world over live in enormous cities. This makes us value flowers even more. Flowers, and especially roses, are 'the language of love'. Flowers are a mark of appreciation or gratitude. Flowers are an expression of kindness. And the nativity shows us that Christ comes to us in kindness.

When my husband and I were working in St Petersburg a friend from Scotland sent us the following letter:

The most eloquent word Jesus had to utter was the Word of his whole life . . . I am, you are, a word spoken by God, a sustaining word. To the suffering world you are a particular word of comfort never to be spoken again. Many people for their entire lives, and most people at some time, know the experience of being cut off by pain, imprisoned by circumstances or by their own personality, and where, oh where is the gentle Christ who promises to bear our burdens? If we look for a Galilean in long robes, we will look in vain. But lots of other people enter our lives, and we must keep reminding ourselves that Christ is coming in them.

Christ comes to us in kindness, for kindness is a grace. We bring a little of the Shekinah, the glory of God, into our cold world when we light candle flames of warmth and goodness for each other. Whether cave or stable, the birthplace of Jesus was filled with light. Shepherds and kings were drawn to that light, then and now.

## People on the fringes

'Now there were in the same country shepherds living out in the fields, keeping watch over their flocks by night' (Luke 2.8).

Working men from the hills were the first to came to the stable. They had been overawed by the angels, but they were perfectly at home in the byre. Western Christianity has equated Christianity with 'respectability' for so long that the Church has often missed out on people on the fringes. The roots of this lie in the social conditions spawned by the industrial revolution. In 1851, Henry Mayhew, a sociologist, conducted a vast survey of London life. He discovered that teenage out-of-wedlock pregnancies were the norm in the east end of London. And despite vast church buildings, chapels and mission halls, Mayhew found that young people were not sure who Jesus was, nor what religious language like 'redemption' meant.

'God almighty made the world, and the poor bricklayers' labourers built the houses arterwards – that's my opinion, but I can't say, for I've never been in no schools,' commented a sixteen year old barrow boy. 'I have heard a little about our Saviour – they seem to say he were a goodish kind of man; but if he says as how a cove's to forgive a feller as hits you, I should say he know'd nothing about it.' (Mayhew, 1985)

Statistics for the twenty-first century show that the divide between affluence and the marginalized is increasing. Let us stay with that for a moment and as we linger in the birthplace of the Lord of kings, let us ponder poverty.

Poverty is – being old and alone with a flickering screen which shows a world which has shut you out. Poverty is – the family forced to relinquish the child they cannot care for. Poverty is – neighbours whose violence you fear. Poverty is – sleeping rough. Poverty is – dying from illness people in the more affluent area up the road recover from. Poverty is – hopelessness. Poverty alienates. Poverty is – for saints. The poor are frowned on when they try to escape from the pressures of daily life by blowing their benefits on a mad purchase or a holiday.

Poverty is powerlessness. It is waiting in dreary offices for unsympathetic officials who have heard it all before and who tell you all the reasons why they cannot help. And then, because you are less articulate or more wounded than they, you get noisy and aggressive and they brand you with two searing words: 'these people'. Those short but condemnatory words distance, deny and despise those to whom they refer.

## The sleeping baby, the hope of Israel

The Gospels challenge us to face up to facts it is sometimes easier to dismiss. Our Christmas cards show a sanitized stable, but we must remember that the shepherds came to the byre in their working clothes. They smelt of sweat and animals and Miriam welcomed them just as they were. They crowded around the animals' feeding trough, where they verified the heaven-sent news. 'For there is born to you this day in the city of David, a Saviour, who is Christ the Lord. And this shall be a sign to you: You will find a babe wrapped in swaddling cloths, lying in a manger' (Luke 2.11–12).

And we may ponder, which of the two marvels is the greater? The angelic host which gave simple men specific signs, or the sleeping baby, the hope of Israel?

Birth – they were used to the ragged scarf of blood across the hillside, the frail bleating which pulsed with new life. But in this scrap of babyhood lying on the hay were encompassed all the hopes and longings of their people and here, before their very eyes, the shepherds saw the salvation proclaimed by the prophets.

The birth took place in Bethlehem because far away in Rome the emperor who called himself Augustus had decreed a census. But the child born in that despised and far-flung rebellious corner of the empire was about to topple the Caesars from their thrones. It had all been fore-told in the Scriptures. The Messiah, God's anointed one, born of David's line, would 'take the ends of the earth for his possession . . . and break them with a rod of iron' (Psalm 2.9). History is about power – as Miriam pointed out in her song. Kings create soaring cathedrals in stone and gold. The poor leave little behind them. Tradition has it that the shepherds left a sheepskin covering for the baby; that they left a lamb for the one who was called the Lamb of God.

The story of Miriam's birth-giving in a byre is a story for all times, for all places – and for all people. If Jesus had been born a prince in courts of power and privilege (as the wise men mistakenly thought) he could never have touched the hearts of common folk who enshrined his birth in carols and hymns. Our oldest carols, strong and unsentimental as they are, show the strength of feeling with which unlettered people welcomed the infant Saviour, how completely they were able to identify with God who came as an infant with no clothes to cover him, no fire to keep him warm.

> Poor little Jesus,
> naked and bare,
> for his poor Mother
> has no covers to share.
> Has no cloth for his bed
> so she cuts up her shawl,
> makes a pillow for his head
> to cover the straw,
> his cold little toes

she rubs and makes warm;
a bitter wind blows
and he sleeps in a barn. . .
(*Jezus malusienki*, Polish traditional carol)

Christmas songs are piped through supermarkets. Let us listen for words which remind us of the tumbledown barn, with a star slanting through ramshackle rafters. As we reflect further upon it we shall see that the hard bare place of birth is linked with the hard bare place of death, that the straw which pricked the body of the infant Jesus prefigured the nails of the cross. In the seventeenth century John Donne wrote, 'all that Christ did or suffered, concurred to our salvation; as well his mother's swathing him in little clouts as Joseph's shrouding him in a funeral sheet; as well his cold lying in the manger as his cold dying on the Cross' (Kenneth, 1983).

## To ponder

Can our faith ever be 'respectable' when the 'Lord of Kings' was homeless? Christ comes to us in kindness, for kindness is a grace. We bring a little of the Shekinah, the glory of God, into our cold world when we light candle flames of warmth and goodness for each other. This 'candle' may be our prayer in the joy of a happy home. It may be something we light in the pain of relationships gone wrong. Is there a little flame, a single prayer-word which might have special meaning for you?

Reflect: Poverty is powerless – poverty is born in a stable and sleeps on hay.

CHAPTER 4

# Waiting is action

◆

## Offering doves

'Now when the days of her purification according to
the law of Moses were completed, they brought him to
Jerusalem to present him to the Lord . . . and to offer a sacrifice according to what is said in the law of the Lord'
(Luke 2.22–24). Miriam carried her six-week-old baby
carefully into the temple. All this, as Luke is at pains to
point out, is exactly according to the law.

> The LORD gave Moses the following regulations for the
> people of Israel. For seven days after a woman gives birth
> to a son, she is ritually unclean . . . On the eighth day
> the child shall be circumcised. Then it will be 33 more
> days before she is ritually clean . . . When the time of
> her purification is completed . . . she shall bring to the
> priest . . . a one-year-old lamb for a burnt offering and
> a pigeon or a dove for a sin offering . . . If the woman
> cannot afford a lamb, she shall bring two doves or two
> pigeons, one for a burnt offering and the other for a sin
> offering. (Leviticus 12.1–8, GNB)

Miriam brought two doves. Doves, the gift of the poor,
were a good offering for the prince of peace who would

49

not ride in triumph on a warhorse, but on a donkey like any peasant farmer. Mary's son fulfils the prophecy of Zechariah: 'Rejoice greatly, O daughter of Zion! Shout, O daughter of Jerusalem! Behold, your King is coming to you; he is just and having salvation, lowly and riding on a donkey, a colt, the foal of a donkey' (Zechariah 9.9).

Moreover, the Holy Spirit would be seen coming from heaven like a dove to nestle upon Jesus (Matthew 3.16). Perhaps, growing up in Nazareth, Jesus would run through the hills, following the flight of a homecoming dove. He would certainly watch pigeons settle upon flat roofs where women ground grain. Each week, when the Sabbath ended, women got out their heavy grindstones and pigeons flocked greedily around, eager for corn after the Sabbath rest.

But now, brought for the first time into the great religious centre which dominates the life of his people, Jesus, a first-born son, is to be consecrated to the Lord according to the law (Exodus 13.2, 13). The covenant of God has already been incised upon his body (Luke 2.21). The Church which would later adore the five wounds of Christ, would conceal the scar of circumcision on the crucified Lord with a mandatory loincloth. This was a mark of respect – but it resulted in denial which would lead to bloodshed and to bitterness which endures to this day.

## Simeon and Anna: the song and the sword

As the ceremony of thanksgiving is performed an old man hurries into the temple.

This is Simeon. Although, as the parables of Jesus will show, many priests were not spiritual men, but self-servers,

Simeon is good and God-fearing, a man who is waiting for the salvation the Messiah will bring. He has already received a promise from the Holy Spirit that, old and frail though he is, he will not die before he sees the Lord's Messiah, the consolation of Israel.

There were no angelic messengers for Simeon, no guiding star, only his faithful waiting and trust. The Holy Spirit prompts him to come into the temple at exactly the right moment. Simeon realizes at once who Jesus is. We may imagine his joy as he takes the child from Miriam and pours out heartfelt praise and gratitude, declaring that this child is indeed Yeshua, the salvation of Israel and the desire of all nations. He will shine like a light for Jews and Gentiles alike. The parents were more than a little awestruck, but this was yet another confirmation of the truth of the angel's words, 'that Holy One who is to be born is the Son of God'. Luke writes, 'And Joseph and his mother marvelled greatly at those things which were spoken of him' (Luke 2.33).

Simeon blesses the parents of the holy child – but the joy of the old man's song turns sharply to sorrow. His blessing for Miriam contained a warning: 'This child is destined for the fall and rising of many in Israel, and for a sign which will be spoken against,' he prophesies, and adds, 'Yes, a sword will pierce through your own soul also' (Luke 2.34–35).

God's love is concerned with wholeness, but here are words of destruction and pain. We cannot separate them from this story: they are there from beginning to end. The risen Lord will be known by his wounds. Broken bread is his sign. We look for success. Jesus shows us brokenness. As we have seen, this is the mystery of mysteries and it was

51

being steadily woven into the life-experience of Miriam of Nazareth. The young mother who has felt the touch of God in her life and is 'blessed among women' must learn to bear the strange blessing of sorrow. I began to understand this when at a time of great personal sorrow a friend sent me words from Ignatius Loyola: 'Your sorrows are your blessings, for they do shelter you in the wounds of Christ.' Another friend wrote that Rabbi Lionel Blue, the popular broadcaster and writer, is reported to have said that he had learnt that his problems were his spiritual capital and the only doorways to charity and mercy he would ever know.

Simeon's prophecy is the first reference in Luke's Gospel to the sufferings of Christ. It is the first indication that his mother Mary will suffer too. She had sung in her Magnificat of holiness, of mercy and strength. She had expressed the great paradox her son will embody in the Gospel: that those who think they are full are really empty. Like Simeon, Miriam understands that if we acknowledge that it is we who are poor, we shall find that those whom the world calls poor reveal Christ to us in his meekness and triumph. Joseph and his young wife came in poverty and humility to fulfil the commands of the law – and they revealed Christ to Simeon, who had waited so long for this moment. They revealed the child as bearer of peace and salvation and as 'a light to bring revelation to the Gentiles, and the glory of your people, Israel' (Luke 2.32).

The revelation is confirmed by the joyful entrance of the aged prophet, Anna, 'a widow of about eighty-four years, who did not depart from the temple, but served God with fastings and prayers night and day' (Luke 2.37–38). These are the traditional good works of the law. Truly one of the humble poor of Israel, Anna is unable to perform the third good work, almsgiving, but, full of thankfulness, she bears witness 'to all those who looked for redemption in Jerusalem' that the longed-for Saviour has come.

Henry Wansbrough, editor of the New Jerusalem Bible, has pointed out that 'The meeting and prophecy in the temple is the first really clear instance of the careful representation by Luke that men and women have equal value before the Lord, an insistence that runs through his work' (Wansbrough, 1998).

Seven women prophets are named in the Old Testament: Sarah, Miriam, Deborah, Hannah, Abigail, Huldah and Esther. We have already considered Miriam of Nazareth's link with Miriam, Deborah and Hannah. Later we shall include Queen Esther and another woman not mentioned above, the great-grandmother of King David, the foreign woman, Ruth.

Now, at the first public witness to the newborn Saviour, aged Anna's ministry and testimony should have been a guiding light for the Church on the position of women in leadership – and not just in the ladies' auxiliary or guild. Anna shows us that waiting in prayer is important, but she is also a prophet and therefore not simply a silent partner of the priest. She 'gave thanks to the Lord and spoke of him to all those who looked for redemption in Jerusalem' (Luke 2.38).

Much remains to be discussed about the women around Jesus and the implication of this for women in today's Church. Each one in her own right affirms essential aspects of ministry. We may think we have made some progress on this subject in Western Europe, but many women feel it's still too little and very late – and in many other countries in the world women are simply passed over in the churches.

## Waiting is action, mends the things action broke

There would have been nothing remarkable about Miriam and Joseph the day they presented themselves and their child at the temple. But Simeon and Anna both look beyond the simplicity and poverty of Joseph and Miriam. They don't think, 'These people are too poor to provide a suitable home for the Messiah.' Or, 'Galileans from Nazareth! Is the Messiah really to be nurtured among half-breeds and Gentiles, and not in Jerusalem where our religion is pure and unadulterated?' Simeon and Anna, who have waited so long for God to reveal his salvation, simply rejoice.

And if in Anna we see an authoritative role for women, we also see the importance of waiting. We do not know how old Simeon is, but Anna has been widowed since she was about 20, and has spent her whole life in prayer and fasting. Now her long years of waiting have been rewarded.

Waiting is boring, a frustrating waste of precious time, but Bernard of Clairvaux has called it the greatest work there is. The hidden people around Jesus show us that waiting can be fruitful. Waiting ploughs the heart, breaking the soil so that the seeds of God can be sown. Prayerful waiting brings the power of the Holy Spirit to earth, as we see in Acts 1.14: 'These all continued with one accord in prayer and supplication, with the women and Mary the mother of Jesus and with his brothers.'

The Bible has a lot to say about prayerful waiting. Psalm 123 is one of the simplest and most poignant passages of Scripture: 'Unto you I lift up my eyes . . . as the eyes of a maid to the hand of her mistress, so our eyes look to the Lord our God, until he has mercy on us' (Psalm 123.1–2).

Basically, waiting means letting go of our busyness, our agendas, our desire to be in control. We do so in order to let God show us his mercy, as the psalm says. It has been said that many Christians seek fellowship so desperately because we are frightened to confront God on our own.

In actual fact, life is full of moments of waiting. We wait for meetings, for appointments, for buses, for trains. We wait in departure lounges, in queues, in traffic jams. We wait at school gates. The secret is to turn these moments into prayer. Then what is frustrating becomes fruitful. We discover that instead of the waiting period being grindingly boring, God has been with us all the time.

### 'God's waiting-room'

A friend wrote recently how waiting on God changed her whole approach in hospital chaplaincy work:

I was so traumatized at first. I have never liked hospitals so my initial reactions were coloured by this. I found it all very difficult but I decided I must be positive so decided the ward was 'the ante-room to heaven' – or 'God's waiting-room' – and plugged away at this in my mind. Fifteen months on everything has changed for me. I love the old people – and now feel to be close to people when they are so ill or near death is a great privilege. So many lovely things happened. I meet so many godly old people who haven't been to church since childhood but are seeking and need God. I won't ever forget them, however fleetingly our paths crossed.

I'm often amazed at how lovingly and cheerfully young nurses tend the sick and dying. I think that when we see the chronically or terminally sick who lie helpless and apparently 'useless' with, for some, only suffering and loneliness as their lot – we feel threatened. I look back now and see how deeply the reality of my own mortality was brought home to me. The feeling of fear initially is, 'This could happen to me'. But time and experience alter that – love and hope and wisdom are of the spirit and not of the body . . .

This is what Mary of Nazareth shows us as she walks her path through obedience and blessing, sorrow and a joy she could never have anticipated when she accepted the will of the Lord in her life. From her patient path we learn that 'hope and wisdom are of the spirit and not of the body'.

Yet this flies in face of our society which values wealth and achievement. Among the ex-pat community with whom I live in Warsaw are businesspeople whose agenda takes them all over Europe and seems to be infinitely extendable. The turnover rate is so high that no one has time to wait. If you don't make time to have a meal or a coffee with someone, you'll have missed your chance – next week they'll be gone. As one friend put it, 'People work and play until the last minute of their stay – and then they're away!'

At a home group, we listened to a tape which instructed us to sit still for four minutes. One person said that this was the first moment he had been still for days! Yet in this busy world I met a woman who shone with serenity and love, even though her husband's work programme had them both living out of suitcases in hotel rooms for weeks on end. As I got to know her better I discovered that the source of her serenity lay in her life of prayer: a life of simple trust, a discipline of early morning silence and the art of making her surroundings beautiful with a bowl of flowers, a string of beads, a child's drawing. But the centre of it all was silence.

It reminded me that Miriam and Elizabeth, Anna and Simeon show us that such prayerful, silent waiting is productive. Jesus is our prime example, here as in all else. He teaches us that waiting is action – and mends the things action broke. A few words in John's Gospel sum up the value Jesus placed on waiting on God. 'And everyone went to his own house. But Jesus went to the Mount of Olives' (John 7.53—8.1).

We must read between the lines, but we can be sure that Jesus spent that night in prayer. With daylight came conflict and quarrelling as men brought before him a woman caught committing adultery. 'They said to him, "Teacher... Moses in the law commanded us that such should be stoned. But what do you say?"' (John 8.5). And the carpenter, who had mended masts and oars broken by stormy winds, ploughshares shattered by stony soil, stooped, and with his silent waiting mended a woman's life.

The themes of this chapter – the blessing of sorrow, the value of prayerful waiting – don't seem very proactive. They don't fit in with the way many Christians have been taught, certainly since the nineteenth century, that we must evangelize the disadvantaged from a position of Christ-centred strength. The Victorian hymn writer Frances Ridley Havergal put it like this in her hymn 'Lord speak to me':

> Lord, strengthen me, that while I stand
> Firm on the rock and strong in Thee,
> I may stretch out a loving hand
> To wrestlers in the troubled sea . . .
> (Frances Ridley Havergal, 1836–79)

But Jesus did more than just 'stretch out a loving hand'. He left the rock of his Father's presence and 'made himself of no reputation, taking the form of a bondservant, and coming in the likeness of men . . . and became obedient to the point of death, even the death of the cross (Philippians 2.7–8). The strength of the Son of God lay in weakness, as we see in the manger in Bethlehem. In Luke's Gospel we read a story which shows the emphasis Jesus places on the value of waiting:

'Be ready for whatever comes, dressed for action and with your lamps lit, like servants who are waiting for their master to come back from a wedding feast. When he comes and knocks, they will open the door for him at once. How happy are those servants whose master finds them awake and ready when he returns!' (Luke 12.35–37, GNB)

Those servants are 'dressed for action' – yet what are they doing? Nothing. Simply waiting. All their action, all their attention is focused on their master's return. So we, too, may carve out five minutes, an hour, an evening, a day – and simply wait and enjoy being one-to-one with God. Instead of pouring out all our needs and plans, our patient, attentive attitude says, 'I love you'. We can see from the story Jesus told how much the Lord values this attentive waiting. For when the master returns from the wedding and finds his servants ready for him, 'he will take off his coat, ask them to sit down and will wait on them' (Luke 12.38).

### 'A little closer every day'

We may think that the elderly with time on their hands and a full harvest of years would find waiting easy. But no. An old Norman knight in a children's story by Rudyard Kipling called it 'the most grievous work I know'. One elderly lady once told Metropolitan Anthony Bloom of the Russian Orthodox Community in London that she found it hard to concentrate on prayer, but she liked to sit and knit. 'Sit and knit before the Lord,' advised Metropolitan Anthony – and she did, with great enjoyment, for learning the secret of letting go had turned prayer into an adventure.

In his books on prayer, Anthony Bloom quotes an extract from the fable by Antoine de Saint-Exupéry about a little prince who met a fox.

The fox gazed at the little prince for a long time. 'Please, tame me!' he said.

'I want to, very much,' the little prince replied. 'But I have not much time. I have friends to discover, and a great many things to understand.'

'If you want a friend, tame me.'

'What must I do, to tame you?' asked the little prince.

'You must be very patient,' replied the fox. 'First, you will sit down at a little distance from me – like that – in the grass. I shall look at you out of the corner of my eye, and you will say nothing. Words are the source of misunderstandings. But you will sit a little closer every day. . .' (Bloom, 1999)

The art of prayer is to 'sit a little closer every day' – and, as we see, no words are necessary.

The people who first welcomed Jesus had waited with great longing. God honoured their faithfulness, and as he revealed himself to them they burst into prophetic utterances. These are like the first birdsong in a dawn of early spring. The Yorkshire hermit Richard Rolle wrote about the longing love which found expression in song:

In the beginning truly of my conversion and singular purpose I thought I would be like the little bird that for love of its lover longs; but in her longing she is gladdened when he comes that she loves. And joying she sings, and singing she longs, but in sweetness and heat. It is said the nightingale to song and melody all night is given that she may please him to whom she is joined. How mickle more with greatest sweetness to Christ my Jesu should I sing, that is spouse of my soul, by all this present life that is night in regard of clearness to come. (Underhill, 1975)

Best-selling books are written on how to achieve calm. The physical benefits of prayer have been quantified and medically proven! Learning the art of sitting still apparently prevents strokes! But for ourselves, having waited, like Simeon, like Anna, like mother Mary 'in her maiden bliss', we shall find that the fruit of our waiting is that we too have 'worshipped the Beloved with a kiss' (Christina Rossetti, 'In the bleak midwinter').

*Waiting is action*

For if waiting in prayer is action which mends the things action broke, waiting is also worship which springs from the simple intimacy of the heart.

## To ponder

The risen Lord will be known by his wounds . . . consider the blessing of sorrow. Think over moments in your life when waiting has turned out to be fruitful and has led you to a deeper awareness of God.

Mary of Nazareth belonged to the 'humble poor' who trusted the Lord. The prophet Isaiah uses the word 'poor' to refer to the whole of Israel, in exile among strangers. The prophet proclaims: 'The Spirit of the Lord is upon me, because the LORD has anointed me to preach good tidings to the poor' (Isaiah 61.1). At the very start of his public ministry, preaching in the synagogue in Nazareth, Jesus applies these words to himself (Luke 4.16–21). But by the time of the coming of Christ 'poor' had come to mean those people who were poor in material goods but rich in faith, like Miriam herself, Elizabeth, Simeon. I wonder how we can weave the gospel truth about 'the poor' into our own Christian lives and our path of prayer?

CHAPTER 5

# A star, three gifts – and flight into Egypt

Mary of Nazareth welcomed scholars as well as shepherds to her humble dwelling place in Bethlehem. So far we have only considered Luke's account of the birth stories. It is time to turn to the Gospel of Matthew. Unlike Luke, Matthew focuses not on Mary but on Joseph, not on Nazareth but on Bethlehem. We shall look more closely at Joseph's role in the next chapter. For now we shall consider the astrologers, or wise men, who saw the Lord's star rise in the east and set out on their camels to worship the newborn king. Muffled against winds which blew grit into their faces, the wise men followed a star, travelling in tracks of old trade paths which had criss-crossed the desert from time immemorial. By day they rested beside their kneeling camels, talking about their libraries, their learning, their charts, talking of the stars and their courses.

Tradition has it that because three gifts are mentioned, there were three sages, from the Orient, from Africa and the North. Thus, the three wise men represent all humanity in our age-old quest for God. Matthew's Gospel will end with the words, 'Go . . . and make disciples of all nations', so perhaps it's not surprising that the opening chapters should show the representatives of 'all nations' seeking the infant king.

Matthew writes: 'Now after Jesus was born in Bethlehem of Judea in the days of Herod the king, behold, wise men from the East came to Jerusalem, saying, "Where is he who is born King of the Jews? For we have seen his star in the East and have come to worship him"' (Matthew 2.1–2).

Like the wise men, we too have a guiding star. God gives us the promise of his presence: 'Your Father knows the things you have need of before you ask him', Jesus assures us (Matthew 6.8).

Miriam took this truth on trust when she consented to the will of the Lord brought to her by the angel. It is the very deep truth which lies at the heart of the family prayer Jesus taught us. We are actually invited to call him 'Dad' or 'Daddy'! Jesus teaches, 'when you pray say, "Abba, Our Father"'. Raniero Cantalamessa, a Roman Catholic theologian, has said that just as the word 'Daddy' brings a young father all the joy of paternity, the Father-heart of God also rejoices to hear the tender, family name. He goes on to say that Jesus knew this and that is why he prayed in this way. The intimate, childish word 'Abba', from Galilee, thus becomes our very own. When we use it we echo the inflexions of the Lord's own Aramaic language.

Our 'star', then, is the promise that God is with us and knows what we need before we ask – and it is also the very name by which we are invited to address God. The difficulty is that the world we inhabit is not very kind to faith, and particularly the kind of faith that 'lets go and lets God'. Nevertheless, like the wise men, we may leave our normal supports behind and travel by the night of unknowing, following the star of God's love on a personal, inner journey to find the child of Bethlehem. For example, St John of the Cross (who died in 1591) described how he left his room at night and climbed a secret stair. He found that the darkness surrounding him was a clearer guide than the light of day. It is from this experience that John of the Cross wrote of 'the dark night of the soul'. Jesus, too, affirms the value of the secret place. 'When you pray, go into your room, and when you have shut your door, pray to your Father who is in the secret place and your Father who sees in secret will reward you openly' (Matthew 6.6). In case we feel confused by the word 'reward', it may be helpful to note that some Bible experts explain that this word means not payment, but a gift freely given.

The trouble is, we may not have a room of our own! Home is often the last place on earth where we can be at peace. The phone rings. The family crash in. Television blares, music beats, the dog is sick, the dinner boils over and someone comes to the door. Don't worry! Way back in the fourteenth century a woman asked a spiritual counsellor, Walter Hilton, how to deepen her prayer life. The wise director of souls advised her not to be vexed at interruptions, but to find God in the neighbour who has just come to the door:

> Father, if someone comes to see me when I am at prayer, help me to see that in leaving you to speak to this stranger, I have not left you at all. I will find you, possess you and see you as fully in this other person as I do when I am praying, although it will be in a different way. (Robertson, 1990)

Mary of Nazareth also found God in her neighbour. She did not turn the shepherds away from the stable, and when the wise men came she showed them the child they sought.

As we hear the music of Matthew's story and ponder its meaning, let us recall that it was not in the courts of the king, but in the gentle welcome of mother Mary that the wise men finally found the child and were filled with 'exceedingly great joy':

> When they heard the king, they departed; and behold, the star which they had seen in the East went before them, till it came and stood over where the young child was. When they saw the star, they rejoiced with exceedingly great joy. And when they had come into the house, they saw the young child with Mary his mother and fell down and worshipped him. And when they had opened their treasures, they presented gifts to him: gold, frankincense and myrrh. (Matthew 2.9–11)

The wise men may have wondered whether God had really guided them to the right place. The poverty of Miriam, the homeless mother, challenges the very basis of our society – and must have disturbed the sages from the East. But they trust the guiding star, and bow their heads low in the dust before the baby, even though the holy family are so humbly housed. Their single guttering flame (oil is expensive and must be used with thrift) shines on the gold the first sage offers – and now Miriam understands that her child is to be a king.

Then the smell of frankincense, fragrant sticky resin which was burnt before the altar in the holy of holies at times of prayer, mingles with the animal smells of the place in which they stay. 'I worship God in this child', was the meaning of the second visitor's gift.

Miriam, woman of the covenant, would have known the

words in Isaiah: 'Kings . . . shall bow down to you with their faces to the earth' (Isaiah 49.23). She must have watched in wonder as the men who were rich and mighty, who had come from the far corners of the earth, worshipped her son. One of God's humble poor, she may have known that the psalms predicted such worship of the promised king:

> The kings of Tarshish and of the isles will bring presents; the kings of Sheba and Seba will offer gifts. Yes, all kings shall fall down before him; all nations shall serve him. For he will deliver the needy when he cries, the poor also and him who has no helper. He will spare the poor and the needy. He will redeem their life from oppression and violence . . . and the gold of Sheba will be given to him. (Psalm 72.10–15)

The third stranger brings myrrh for the Messiah who will die for the life of the world. And now, perhaps, the young mother shrinks back in dismay, for myrrh, precious myrrh, was used at a burial, and one black day she will hold her son's body in her arms. She will tuck myrrh into the folds of his shroud: 'And Nicodemus, who at first came to Jesus by night, also came, bringing a mixture of myrrh and aloes, about a hundred pounds. Then they took the body of Jesus, and bound it in strips of linen, as the custom of the Jews is to bury' (John 19.39–40).

St Peter Chrysologus, a medieval writer, described the visit of the magi in a way which points up the mystery of 'God in man' and the meaning of the three gifts:

Today the Magus, the wise man, finds weeping in a crib him whom he sought for shining in the stars. Today the wise man reveres clearly revealed in swaddling clothes him whom he had long patiently awaited unseen in the heavens. Today the wise man ponders in profound amazement over what he sees there: heaven on earth, earth in heaven, man in God, God in man, and him whom the whole universe cannot contain confined in a tiny boy. And immediately on seeing he professes with mystical gifts that he believes and does not argue: he acknowledges God with frankincense, the King with gold, with myrrh the mortal one destined to die. (Kenneth, 1983)

The mysterious magi have brought gifts – but they have not yet learnt the truths Miriam has expressed in her song. In the last chapter we reflected that wisdom is of the spirit, not of the body. The sages had assumed that the child born to save the world would be cradled in the place of power and so they mistakenly sought the baby in the courts of King Herod – where they stirred up a hornets' nest. Often, in our ignorance, we make mistakes which cause us great anxiety and may even do serious harm. Perhaps in the darkness it would be good to turn back to this story and see how God is able to work out his purposes in spite of our mistakes. He saves Jesus from Herod's soldiers, although (and it is a very hard 'although') other baby boys under two are murdered.

## The slaughter of little children

The night is torn apart by crying – the slaughter of the

children. The massacre provides a New Testament parallel with the slaughter of the baby boys in Egypt which opens the book of Exodus: 'Now there arose a new king over Egypt, who did not know Joseph. And he said to his people, "Look, the people of the children of Israel are more and mightier than we; come, let us deal shrewdly with them, lest they multiply"' (Exodus 1.8–10).

Ethnic cleansing is nothing new. Tragically, statistics show that violent crimes against ethnic minorities are on the increase across Europe. The causes are exactly the same as they were in Old Testament times: fears and insecurities are projected on to foreign workers who cover labour and skill shortages, often doing jobs nationals don't want, as the Hebrew slaves in Egypt did. The incident in the book of Exodus brings on stage those two splendid dissidents, Shiphrah and Puah, who defied Pharaoh's order to murder baby boys at birth. The two Hebrew midwives 'feared God and . . . saved the male children alive' (Exodus 1.15–21), and with great courage and quick-wittedness explained their political disobedience in terms which brought credit to their oppressed people.

> So the king of Egypt called for the midwives and said to them, 'Why have you done this thing, and saved the male children alive?' And the midwives said to Pharaoh, 'Because the Hebrew women are not like the Egyptian women; for they are lively and give birth before the midwives come to them.' Therefore God dealt well with the midwives, and the people multiplied and grew very mighty. (Exodus 1.18–20)

The massacre of infant boys described in the Gospel of Matthew is in keeping with the character of Herod whom the historian Josephus described as 'brutish, and a stranger to all humanity'. He had three of his own sons put to death and his cruelty was proverbial. During Herod's tyrannical reign, said Josephus, no woman's virtue and no man's life was safe.

Nor, we know from the Gospel, were the lives of little children. Incensed by the apparent duplicity of the magi, who were warned by God 'that they should not return to Herod' (Matthew 2.12), the murderous king sent soldiers through Bethlehem and the surrounding countryside with orders to kill all baby boys under the age of two. Matthew reminds us that Old Testament prophecies are being fulfilled. He quotes the prophet Jeremiah: 'A voice was heard in Ramah . . . Rachel, weeping for her children, refusing to be comforted, because they were no more' (Matthew 2.18).

Mother Rachel was to weep for her children through many more slaughters, until at last, shockingly, in the twentieth century the words were to be almost literally fulfilled. Almost, but not quite. Whole families, whole communities, whole orphanages, whole hospitals, whole overcrowded trainloads of deported people were murdered, but Israel did not die. A remnant survived to bear witness to the crime, to start life again.

## A refugee, thrown on the charity of strangers

As Herod's soldiers attacked tiny children, all Bethlehem was astir, horrified. But the holy family are safe: '. . . an angel of the Lord appeared to Joseph in a dream, saying, "Arise, take the young child and his mother, flee to Egypt, and stay there until I bring you word; for Herod will seek the young child to destroy him"' (Matthew 2.13).

So Jesus began his life as a refugee, thrown on the

charity of strangers. But from now on foreigners too will hear the voice of God. The kingdom is being extended to include the Gentiles. 'I will gather all nations and tongues, and they shall come and see my glory,' says the Lord (Isaiah 66.18). Matthew's account gives a dramatic impression of the despotic power of the reigning monarch, while the child, the king of kings, seems weak and helpless. But this is not the case. The child Jesus is centre stage. This is his story and the focus is entirely on him. His weakness and vulnerability embody the truth of his mother's praise poem: 'He has scattered the proud in the imagination of their hearts. He has put down the mighty from their thrones, and exalted the lowly' (Luke 1.51–52). King Jesus, not Herod, will conquer. But first he must travel the path of helplessness and humility, a refugee, thrown on the charity of foreigners. For the holy family are forced to flee; and in our own day we see them again and again in homeless and hopeless families fleeing Bosnia, Rwanda, Chechnya . . .

Yet, we must stress, this is not defeat. Egyptian Christians are proud that the holy family took refuge in their land. Coptic Christians actually date the beginnings of their ancient Church from the flight into Egypt.

In the most ancient icons of the virgin and child, painted on wood or carved in stone from Ethiopia to Ireland, from Egypt to the Hebrides, from Syria to Russia, the mother is shown as a throne on which her infant son is elevated and from which he blesses the world. The mother is shown as the temple wherein we find the holy child. He is its centre, the seat of such profound wisdom that his brow is rounded like a dome, radiating light, dignity and an immense and ancient sense of serenity. So, as we picture the holy family departing to Egypt, we may imagine them guarded by angels and protected so securely by the Father's love that the child travels in his mother's arms like a prince on a royal throne.

The little family leave by night. An Egyptian prayer from the third century says: 'The Lord, once the Scourge of monarchs, now, fleeing from the evil king, escapes by night to Egypt.' Coptic Christians, drawing parallels between the Old and New Testaments, remind us that it was also by night that the Pharaoh called Moses and his brother Aaron and told them, 'Go!' It was by night, too, that the people of Israel fled in haste from the Egyptians (Exodus 12.30, 31–41).

Egypt, the land of the pharaohs, with its ancient civilization, featured in the pages of the Bible as a place of refuge and help, as well as of oppression. Indeed, the references to Egypt are so many that when they are listed in small print in a Bible concordance they fill five and a half columns, each 24 centimetres in length.

In the first half of the first book of the Bible we read: 'Now there was a famine in the land, and Abram went down to Egypt to dwell there, for the famine was severe in the land' (Genesis 12.10). Later in the same book we read how Joseph, the favoured son of the patriarch Jacob, was taken to Egypt as a slave – but became governor under Pharaoh and opened the storehouses of Egypt to starving peasant farmers of his homeland, including his brothers (Genesis 37—46). Finally, the aged Jacob journeyed to Egypt, where Pharaoh gave him and his offspring land (Genesis 47).

However, as we have seen, when the Hebrews grew very numerous, the pharaohs oppressed them, making them slave labourers on huge building works which still draw tourists from all over the world. And in the end, under Moses, they had to flee from Egypt (Exodus 1—14).

The Lord brought ten plagues upon Egypt, but that was by no means the end of the story. King Solomon, 'whose wisdom excelled even the wisdom of Egypt' (1 Kings 4.30), made a treaty with Pharaoh and married Pharaoh's daughter (1 Kings 3.1). Jeroboam, a future king of Israel, fled to Egypt from Solomon (1 Kings 11.40) and the prophet Jeremiah was taken there in captivity (Jeremiah 43.6).

Egypt exerts an enduring fascination for people. Children 'do' ancient Egypt in school. Exhibits from the pyramids draw vast crowds. The River Nile, as the Greek historian Herodotus pointed out, gave birth and breath to the very beginnings of civilization. From being nomadic hunters, people began to settle around the ground made fertile by the regular flooding of the river which gave them their grain and fish, their seasons and their calendar. The Egyptians developed hieroglyphic or picture writing as far back as 3000 BC, opening the windows into the mindset of this fascinating civilization.

Obsessed with immortality, they regarded death as a passing on into another sphere of life. Archaeologists have unearthed a very early burial. The body was placed in the foetal position, ready for new birth. But the passage to the 'other world' was preceded by judgement. The gods held scales weighted with a feather on one side, and on the other the heart of the one who had died. Sin made the heart heavy, and if it outweighed the feather, the consequences were not pleasant! So vital was the heart that even though all other organs were removed when a corpse was mummified, the heart was left.

The rich civilization of the pharaohs eventually crumbled. The Old Testament shows us that the Hebrew prophets rebuked the rulers of Israel and Judah for allying themselves with the Egyptians. Jeremiah predicted disaster for Egypt from the Babylonians. All the statues of gods in the temple will be shattered (43.11–13), he prophesied. He also predicted doom for the Jewish communities which had been deported to Egypt but persisted in offering sacrifices to the 'queen of heaven', the Babylonian goddess Ishtar (44.1–30).

## 'Blessed is Egypt my people'

But Egyptian Christians point out that Scripture also predicts that the Lord will heal Egypt and bless the land:

> And the LORD will strike Egypt, he will strike it and heal it; they will return to the LORD, and he will be entreated by them and heal them . . . In that day Israel will be one of three with Egypt and Assyria – a blessing in the midst of the land, whom the Lord of hosts shall bless, saying, 'Blessed is Egypt my people, and Assyria the work of my hands, and Israel my inheritance.' (Isaiah 19.22, 24–25)

If the Lord calls Egypt 'my people', Syria 'the work of my hands', Israel 'my inheritance', might there not be in God's plan a blueprint for peace in the Middle East which politicians have not dreamed of? A genuine holy peace among the People of the Book, Muslim, Jew, Christian – Orthodox, Coptic, Catholic, Protestant – could arise from understanding these Scriptures and respecting our differing approaches to them.

Christianity in Egypt is very ancient. Recently I was privileged, by means of video, lectures, slides, posters and a CD, to make a 'tour' of Christian Egypt from the viewpoint of Christians from the Coptic Church, one of the oldest forms of Christianity. I should like to share it with you, as I believe there is much we can learn from exploring a form of Christianity which is so ancient, but which is also little known in the West.

I can remember when Western Reformed Christians doubted that Coptic believers really were Christians! There is now a Coptic parish in Scotland, St Mark's in Kirkcaldy, across the Forth Bridge from Edinburgh. They have taken over a disused Church of Scotland building and made it their own, adding icons and an iconostasis – the stand for icons which separates the inner sanctuary from the congregation. They copied the designs from some of their best-loved churches from home, just as British people abroad built churches like the ones they had left behind.

The priest and people of St Mark's Coptic Church held an exhibition of their traditions and worship in Edinburgh. I was struck by the warmth and welcome I was given, by a deep appreciation of holiness and by the love of the people for their ancient Christian traditions, which date back to the dawn of Christianity. One legend says that St Mark brought the new faith to Egypt in AD 41. Weary, walking around the city of Alexandria, Mark broke his sandal and went into a sandal-maker's shop. Just at that moment the sandal-maker pricked his finger. Mark healed him in the name of the Lord and won his first convert.

Legend often has truth at its core. The truth is that Alexandria was an important trade centre, and the Gospel probably spread south from that city, with its large Jewish community. Bible scholars also think it is likely that the holy family took refuge among the Jewish community in Alexandria, but the Coptic Church has a different version, as we shall hear in a moment. Meantime, here are a few more facts about this ancient church.

The Bible was translated into Coptic (the language of Egypt) at a very early date: towards the end of the second century, around AD 200. At about that time the name of God replaced the names of the pharaohs on inscriptions still to be seen in crumbling temples. Fifty years or so later saw the first martyrs. Pagan Egypt, like Rome, was basically tolerant of other gods and would happily have added the Lord Jesus to its pantheon. But Christianity demands a higher place for the Christ and when the emperors demanded sacrifice in return for a certificate of citizenship, Christians stood out as dissenters. The calendar of the Coptic Christian Church, one of the most ancient of all Christian churches, dates from 284 when, under the Emperor Diocletian, massacres of martyrs took place. In fact, although the earliest recorded martyrdoms took place in Rome under the Emperor Nero, Africa was a very early scene of Christian witness; the deaths of Perpetua and Felicity and their companions in Carthage around 202 precede those in Egypt.

Christians under pressure took refuge in ancient temples, where they built secret centres of worship. A Christian cross is still visible in a temple once dedicated to the goddess Isis, and worship continued at that spot until the sixth century. Fading frescoes in other temples also tell the story. Archaeologists have uncovered five saints depicted in a niche in an old temple of the pharaohs. In another,

Christians defaced old idols and chopped up a group statue of gods to form a cross.

Egypt therefore boasts an unbroken Christian tradition right back to the very earliest days of the infant Church. Indeed, Coptic missionaries are said to have taken the Christian faith to Ireland.

But with the flight of the holy family to Egypt, Coptic Christians claim a blessing unique among the Gentile nations: their land was given the honour of sheltering the child. The verses in Isaiah 25, 'Blessed is Egypt my people . . .', are taken to refer directly to the flight into Egypt. A film by the Egyptian Tourist Board commented very beautifully, 'The holy family cross the Sinai desert guided only by the stars, the light of the heavens to the pure in heart.' The commentary continued: 'Every place that the Virgin Mary and Jesus set foot on has become holy and blessed.' This note of respect and reverence encouraged me to follow the Coptic version of the flight into Egypt.

## On a swift cloud

'Behold the LORD rides on a swift cloud, and will come into Egypt. The idols of Egypt will totter at his presence, and the heart of Egypt will melt in its midst.' This text, Isaiah 19.1, is quoted by Coptic Christians as referring directly to the arrival of the infant Christ in Egypt. The text is glossed in an ancient prayer: 'Who is the swift cloud? It is the Virgin Mary.'

The virgin herself is said to have dictated the itinerary of the journey to a priest–monk, Pope Theophilis. ('Pope' is used in a more general way in the Coptic Church than we use it in the West.) The journey can be precisely dated, lasting for three and a half years, and the itinerary is quite specific. Here is a brief outline of the story as tradition records it. For safety reasons, the holy family could not follow the usual trade routes, so the angel led them a different way. There was no place for them to rest and so the words of Jesus are applied in the Coptic tradition to the travels of the infant Christ and his family in Egypt: 'Foxes have holes and birds of the air have nests, but the Son of Man has nowhere to lay his head' (Luke 9.58).

The holy family are said to have slept in caves – sometimes sharing their shelter with lions. Sometimes townspeople welcomed them into their city and the infant Jesus blessed that place and its people. Many historic churches trace their foundation to that holy moment when ancient idols were shattered and the infant Christ was honoured instead: in these instants historical truth and Christian legend intermingle.

The whole journey was fraught with danger from wild animals, Roman soldiers and bandits. At one point bandits fell upon the holy family and robbed them. Did they carry off the wise men's precious gifts of gold, frankincense and myrrh, one wonders? Pope Theophilis doesn't tell us, but says that one bandit felt sorry for what he had done and returned the stolen goods. It is said that this bandit was the good thief who was later crucified with Christ.

When there was no water, Mary wept – and water flowed, and Mary bathed her child and washed his clothes. Our own folk tradition also tells us that speedwells, the small blue flowers which grow in summer meadow and on sunlit headland, are the virgin's tears which she shed on the flight to Egypt. The little flowers, like miniature stars, guide the traveller – hence the name 'speed well'. Thus

Mary's tears turned to tokens of blessing for every traveller, while Egypt is transported to the Hebrides, where holy St Bride is said to have nursed the fosterling so that the mother might rest upon her way.

Although this is the stuff of legend, there are biblical truths to be found here. Hospitality to strangers and way-farers brings blessing. The travel-worn fugitive family, united in their care for one another, accepted hospitality meekly, and repaid it with blessing. We have already thought about the value of blessing one another. The Lord had said long ago to Abram, 'I will bless those who bless you' (Genesis 12.3). Isaiah, as we have seen, predicts bless-ing for Egypt, the chosen refuge for the Son. 'Blessed is Egypt my people . . .' has a special resonance for Egyptian Christians. They find great consolation in the fact that after the ten plagues in the book of Exodus, God did not close the door of mercy and kept blessing Egypt through the ages. The holy family came as fugitives and Egypt did not turn them away, so some Egyptian Christians find a special promise for their nation in John's Gospel: 'as many as received him, to them he gave the right to become children of God, to those who believe in his name' (John 1.12).

Coptic Christians worship the Lord in ways which seem unfamiliar to Western Christians. The liturgy is long and complicated, heavily overlaid with symbolism. For example, at baptism the naked baby is plunged three times into water and is anointed with oil. Then, dried and clothed in white with a scarlet ribbon bound around its breast (a symbol of salvation), the infant receives communion, a morsel of bread soaked in wine. It is believed that this ceremony has made the child a full member of Christ's church, baptized and confirmed, with the indwelling of the Spirit symbolized by the anointing with oil.

Coptic churches are ornate. Incense is copiously shaken. The liturgy comments:

> This is the golden censer, containing fragrant incense, held in the hands of Aaron the priest, who offers it upon your altar. The golden censer is the Virgin, while the incense cloud is the Saviour. She has carried him who has saved us and forgives our sins. The censer of pure gold carries live coals of fire. (Day, 1972)

This brief exploration cannot do justice to an ancient tradition, but the place given to the holy family by the Coptic Church is worth pondering.

## To ponder

> Egypt . . . will return to the LORD, and he will be entreated by them and heal them . . . In that day Israel will be one of three with Egypt and Assyria – a blessing in the midst of the land, whom the Lord of hosts shall bless, saying, 'Blessed is Egypt my people, and Assyria the work of my hands, and Israel my inheritance.' (Isaiah 19.22, 24–25)

Pray for blessing and peace in the Middle East. Unfortunately, Bethlehem and other Bible place names are mentioned so often in our news as scenes of continuing violence. We listen with sorrow – but we can also listen with prayer, asking the Lord for his mercy, praying for the peace of Jerusalem:

Jerusalem is built as a city that is compact together, where the tribes go up, the tribes of the LORD . . . Pray for the peace of Jerusalem: 'May they prosper who love you. Peace be within your walls, prosperity within your palaces' . . . Because of the house of our Lord, I will seek your good. (Psalm 122.3–4, 6–7, 9)

# CHAPTER 6

# Joseph, the foster-father, 'worker of the hard wood'

———◆———

The infant Christ was at risk from a despotic tyrant, but the statistics of murder show that it is generally those who are closest to us who are most likely to do us harm. This is a disturbing thought, not least because domestic violence (most usually against women and children) is still a suppressed issue in many countries of the world. 'It doesn't happen here,' we are told. And when we press further, the answer invariably is, 'Well, maybe it does happen, but we don't talk about it.' An American study has shown that a child under two who lives with a stepfather or an unrelated male who happens to be 'partnering' the child's mother, is seventy times more likely to be murdered than a child living with its biological father. (*Church Times*, 23 June 2000)

## The lovely word 'foster', the lovely word 'husband'

These statistics show how important the role of foster or adopting fathers is. In many countries of the world it is unthinkable for a man to adopt the product of stranger's seed. However, men who self-sacrificially offer a child at risk a name, a shelter and family life, give them rock-bottom security. Appeals for caring families for children in need are piped through supermarkets, but all too little is said in praise of families who adopt or foster, far less about the fathers.

It is time to turn to Joseph, the foster-father of the Lord, who is pictured in art and sculpture as well as in Scripture in a self-effacing, nurturing, protective role. One of my favourite pieces of woodcarving is of the holy family. Joseph encircles mother and child. He gathers his cloak about them with one hand while with the other he holds up a lantern, lighting their way, watchful for danger. An icon I saw recently also made me pause, for it showed a man holding a child. Who could this be? I wondered. I looked a little more closely and realized that it was Joseph and his foster-son.

In an age when adults move through serial relationships and children may have a succession of men but no one father, this picture of the nurturing foster-father is powerful and healing. I am using the word 'foster' in its widest sense. I think of a father whose new marriage meant taking on the care of two boys, one with learning difficulties. His unselfish acceptance must have helped both sons through the pain of losing their birth-father. And as I write this, I want to thank the father, as well as the mother, who took my granddaughter into their family and made her their own. The concept of the holy family is potentially a source for wholeness in our fragmented, isolated society. Children in foster-care often feel disadvantaged and vulnerable. In fact, we should honour them and let them know that the Son of God was a foster-child also. As many fathers take an increasing role in parenting, while others lose contact with their children because relationships break down, the man who fostered a child not his own and the mother who stood at the foot of the cross both become eloquent models of hope.

We shall explore some of the tensions Miriam experienced in her family life in the next chapter. But as we meditate on her husband, Joseph, the foster-father, I should like to include this extract from a choral piece, written by Brother Aidan Doherty, a member of a Roman Catholic teaching order who had been living and working among the people of Liberia and Sierra Leone for over 30 years when he sent this poem to me:

### Joseph

Call me
Bar Jacob, bar David,
Known to Nazarenes, few else,
Carver of the olive.

Shaper
Of the plough, bowl and bed,
Table, plate, chair and spoon,
Bound to the Lord, his Son,
And my Mary in love.

His, hers
And mine, the aching pain
Of the cross, so slowly dragged
Past Romans, Pharisees,
Who could not understand

That I
Worker of the hard wood
Was also moulded, chiselled
To something beautiful
Carved by the Lord.

(Robertson, 1989)

For Joseph to fulfil the role of foster-father, he had to come to terms with the fact that the girl he was going to marry had suddenly become pregnant. That's a shock for anyone – but this child was so miraculously conceived that theologians past and present still debate whether or not it was possible.

Miriam of Nazareth was unmarried when the great work of the Lord God began within her and she conceived the Saviour of the world. Yet, in spite of our understanding of the blessedness of the unmarried pregnant girl in Nazareth, illegitimacy is still a social stigma; until very recently, an unmarried mother was virtually an outcast. Before the days of widely available contraception – in other words, right into the 1960s, unmarried pregnant girls sought refuge in mother-and-baby homes and were obliged to give up their child immediately for adoption. Or they lived a lie, bought a wedding ring, often at the request of their parents, and pretended to be married. A friend to whom this had happened over 30 years ago broke down when she spoke of it recently. The pain and the hurt were still so real to her, even though her child is an adult and she has received much inner healing. Someone else I know who is very active in his local community told me that he was the child of an unmarried mother. His granny had 'taken him in'. When visitors came he was given a cake or a scone like the other children in the family, but he was sent to his room and told to stay out of sight until the guests had gone. Large working–class families often absorbed an illegitimate child, but very often the young mother was passed off as an aunt or big sister and granny took charge as Mum.

When we understand this stigma we can see how totally Miriam's response to God turned her life upside down. Joseph was not left untouched either. Anxious to preserve intact the virginity of the Mary of the Church before and after her marriage, Christian tradition stated that she was given into the care of an old man. But in fact Joseph was most likely about 18, and certainly no older than 21 or 22. The normal marrying age for Jewish men in Bible times was between late teens and early twenties, and this pattern held good in the small towns of Eastern European Jewry for centuries. The received wisdom was that a young man should be brought beneath the chuppah, the bridal canopy, as soon as the first hair appeared upon his chin.

So we can imagine Joseph, devout and God-fearing, young and in love, longing to be with his young bride; and although some young men hurried to set up home before the 12-month betrothal was over, Joseph was content to wait until the right time came. How shocked he must have been at the news that the young girl to whom he was betrothed had deceived him and was pregnant!

'Don't speak of love,' a woman whispered, 'it vanishes when troubles come . . .' But Joseph's love didn't vanish, although troubles seemed to have come thick and fast. Even in his distress his thoughts were for Miriam, how best to protect her good name and quite literally save her life. The young couple from Nazareth were caught in a double-bind, as Jacob of Serug explained in the sixth century:

> If Mary had revealed the divine mystery, she would have been scorned, hated, calumniated. She would have been slandered, persecuted and stoned; she would have been regarded as an adulteress and a liar. Because of this, divine providence had sought for her a just spouse to be her husband . . . And he brought her into his house, lest they reckon her among the adulteresses . . . Joseph was specially chosen for that matter so that he might be the reputed father of our Lord, at the time of his coming . . . so gossip and ill-repute abated for the daughter of David. (Jacob of Serug, 1995)

Little though Scripture tells us of Joseph, what is revealed is quality stuff! Tossing and turning on his sleeping mat, he decides that the best way out of his predicament is to put an end to his marriage contract in private. He will lose the betrothal money, but Miriam will keep her good name: 'Then Joseph, her husband, being a just man, and not wanting to make her a public example, was minded to put her away discreetly' (Matthew 1.19).

When we use this word 'just' in English today we think of someone who is fair and impartial. In Judaism the concept is wider. A just man, 'ish tzaddik', is a man who is just and righteous because he bases his behaviour upon the law of the Lord. Sadik is used in the same way in Islam as well.

But this deep sense of justice was about to be stretched. All Joseph's compassion and love are going to be called upon. This is the stuff of the gospel. It is this honouring of the law, yet interpreting with mercy its strict requirements, that will be the hallmark of the teaching of Jesus. All his parables teach us that God our heavenly Father has an understanding of justice which is far wider, far deeper than the teaching of the law. And surely this is evidence that the just man, Joseph, taught his foster-son by example, as well as showing him how to be a worker with wood.

Joseph learns this lesson the hard way. It causes him much heart-searching and it requires a visit from an angel before he fully understands: 'But while he thought about these things, behold an angel of the Lord appeared to him in a dream, saying, "Joseph, son of David, do not be afraid to take to you Mary your wife, for that which is conceived in her is of the Holy Spirit"' (Matthew 1.20).

Joseph is therefore asked to look beyond the strict requirements of the law of Moses and to give Miriam and her child his name and protection. He also has to forgo some of his most deeply cherished dreams. For there was no 'wedding night'. Joseph, says Matthew, 'did not know' his young bride 'till she had brought forth her firstborn son' (Matthew 1.25). Joseph was truly being chiselled into 'something beautiful for the Lord'.

Recent surveys have shown that people find that what they gain from church on Sunday helps them in their personal devotion but has very little relevance in the workplace. Here, however, Joseph offers us an example. He was a craftsman (Mark 6.3) who would teach his foster-son his trade. He could mend and fashion masts, oars, ploughs – and with the same patience and self-effacing devotion that he brought to his daily work, Joseph of Nazareth fashioned a secure home for the Son of God, 'Bound to the Lord, his Son, and my Mary in love,' as Brother Aidan's poem puts it.

Yet, apart from Christmas cards, we've edited Joseph out of the story. Let us put him back, and together with him, put back the lovely word 'foster', along with the equally lovely word 'husband'. And, in an age in which sex without procreation is so normal that the word 'partner' has replaced 'spouse', let us hold Joseph up as an example of a man who protected his bride-to-be and embraced and nurtured a child he had not engendered.

## To ponder

Consider Joseph, the carpenter who could mend broken masts, oars, ploughs – and with the same patience and self-effacing devotion created a secure home for the Son of God.

The penalty of adultery was death by stoning. 'The adulterer and the adulteress shall surely be put to death,' says Leviticus 20.10. The book of Deuteronomy adds that 'you shall stone them to death by stones' (Deuteronomy 22.24). Jesus, the child whose conception caused Joseph so much worry, would soften the harsh strictures of the law in defence of a woman caught in adultery (John 8.1–11). 'Moses in the law commanded us that such should be stoned,' said the sticklers for justice. But Jesus 'stooped down and wrote on the ground with his finger as though he did not hear'. Then, as the questioners continued to challenge him, Jesus, the son of Miriam of Nazareth, about whom ill rumour might have spread were it not for the protection of the foster-father, Joseph, said, 'He who is without sin among you, let him throw a stone at her first.' The woman's accusers melted away and Jesus said to her, 'Neither do I condemn you: go and sin no more'. Does the dilemma faced by the carpenter of Nazareth, whose bride-to-be was with child, cast new light on the actions of the foster-son?

# CHAPTER 7

# Family friction and the
# way of faith

---◆---

We have seen that the birth of Jesus in a human family means that in a mysterious way every new family becomes the holy family, no matter what stresses and disappointments later occur. Family life is tough. It is often crucifixion. The sword which Simeon foretold pierces us also, heart and soul. There are no quick answers, no short cuts, but we glimpse new depths to the meaning of mercy.

So, hang on in there, because the very fact that such an ordinary family was chosen as the place of nurture for the Saviour of the world shows us that God is present in greatest joy and greatest need. We understand the joy, all right, but when the need is most acute, it is very hard, even impossible, to see the Lord. The family of Jesus of Nazareth experienced troubles from without and from within, as we shall see. Family friction does not negate the way of faith, even though it takes us to rock-bottom and there often seems no way out.

Sentimentalizing the holy family on Christmas cards is as deceitful as commercial advertisements which show us affluent, smiling, well-groomed adults and children. From its opening pages, the Bible presents us with a devastatingly accurate portrayal of human nature. I realized this when I started to dig into Scripture in order to write Bible stories for children. The Bible is a tough book to explain to young readers! Adam and Eve sinned, Noah exposed himself in a drunken stupor, Abraham passed his wife off as his sister, Jacob the cheat is swindled, Rachel his beloved wife steals her father's household gods and lies to him about it. In fact we get to Joseph before we have a moral, honest character – and he is more than a little boastful and just a touch vain! We hear the disciples quarrelling. Paul and Mark fall out, but make it up in the end. The Bible is definitely not about good people. It is about good things God does through weak, sinful women and men. This is one of many things which gives the Bible the ring of truth: we meet real flesh-and-blood people, not plaster-cast saints with shiny haloes.

## Growing up in Nazareth: the mystery of the commonplace

The Gospels hint at 'the hidden life in Nazareth'. We have seen that foster-father Joseph takes care to teach Miriam's son his trade (Mark 6.3). We can picture the growing boy, planing wood in the carpenter's workshop. The quiet home in Nazareth gives us space to reflect upon the mystery of the commonplace; the miracle of the everyday which prepares the way for so much else in the Gospels. Jesus himself brings simple things into his most intimate life of prayer and shows us how we may do the same, saying 'Abba, Father' and asking for our most basic needs to be met. We shall see how, at the urging of his mother, he changes water into wine. For him the sacred and the secular, the miracle and the homely life of everyday, are so intertwined that he raises Jairus' daughter with the humdrum words of everyday life, 'Talitha cumi: little sister, it's time to get up and have breakfast!'

> When he came in, he said to them, 'Why make this commotion and weep? The child is not dead, but sleeping' . . . Then he took the child by the hand, and said to her, 'Talitha cumi', which is translated, 'Little girl, I say to you arise.' Immediately the girl arose and walked . . . He commanded them strictly that none should know about it, and said that something should be given her to eat. (Mark 5.39, 41–43)

We have already seen that in the 'just man', Joseph, Jesus the foster-son had a daily example of the faith that takes God at his word and submits wholeheartedly. 'Abraham believed God and it was accounted to him for righteousness,' says Paul (Romans 4.3), quoting the book of Genesis. And these words must be applied to mother Miriam too.

## 'My Father's business'

But it's still tough going. The parents are anxious and do not always understand Jesus, as we see during the visit to Jerusalem for the feast of Passover when Jesus is 12 years old.

On the way home, by nightfall, a whole day into their journey, Jesus is missing. It was, apparently, the custom for men and women to travel in two separate groups on the way home from the pilgrimage and so it is easy to see how neither Miriam nor Joseph would have known at first that Jesus was missing: each would think he was with the other.

Once they realize, they search among their relatives – and here we have a picture of the extended family and see, too, how Jesus must have made himself comfortably at home among his cousins and uncles and aunts.

Back in the temple, they find 12-year-old Jesus with the learned doctors of the law, listening and questioning, the twin tools of wisdom. All Miriam's pent-up emotion bursts out in her relief at seeing her son. Every parent who has lain awake in the wee small hours, unable to sleep until the key turns in the lock, knows how fears fuse in a hot tension of relief and fury. 'Son,' cries Miriam, 'why have you done this to us? Your father and I have sought you anxiously.' But Jesus answers, 'Did you not know that I must be about my Father's business?' (Luke 2.49). And Luke comments that they did not understand his reply.

Christians do not always understand Jesus either, so we can identify very well with the perplexed and angry parents who have spent three frantic days searching for their lost son, only to be rebuked by him in unexpected defiance of the fourth commandment – and this in front of the highly educated scholars of the holy city!

Those who pray the rosary will know that 'finding Jesus in the temple' is the fifth part of the joyful mystery. Friends who use a rosary tell me that it is actually a prayerful meditation on the main events in the life of the Lord Jesus, accompanied by his mother. It is a pathway into prayer.

The idea of prayer beads is quite ancient and not specifically Christian. 'Worry beads' are used in the Arab world to soothe the wearer in moments of stress. I've seen travellers in airports with a small bracelet of dark beads around a wrist or slipping between their fingers. The Old English word 'to pray' was 'to bid', and so the link between prayer and beads is rooted in the language. The beads were orig-inally a set of counting devices used as a means of keeping the prayer-flow right. Nowadays nuns wear long black beads at their belts. An early example of a nun with a rosary in English literature is found in Chaucer's *Canterbury Tales*. His simpering, vain Prioress, with her perfect table man-ners, wears her rosary as a decoration 'about hir arm'. The beads are 'of small coral . . . gauded al with grene'. Rosary beads are arranged in groups of ten. Between each set of ten beads is a bigger bead, rather like a full stop, on which you say the creed. Chaucer calls this big bead a 'gaud', and the one on the Prioress' rosary is green. 'Gaud', inci-dentally, comes from the Latin word 'gaudeum', which means 'joy'. It has stayed in our language as 'gaudy' – which Chaucer implies the Prioress' beads certainly were.

Each of the ten small beads represents one 'Hail Mary', a prayer which repeats the salutation of the angel Gabriel: 'Hail Mary, full of grace, the Lord is with you. Blessed are you among women and blessed is the fruit of your womb, Jesus.' If you experiment with a rosary as an aid to prayer, you will feel quite comfortable with that biblical part of the prayer, whatever branch of the Church you belong to. The prayer continues, 'Holy Mary, Mother of God, pray for us sinners now and at the hour of our death.' My friend, who prays a Hail Mary for prisoners condemned to death, finds the second half of the prayer very appropriate in that context.

The sets of beads are linked in a circle which terminates in a small chain with five more beads leading to a crucifix. These beads begin and end the saying of the rosary and represent the Lord's Prayer, three Hail Marys and the Gloria. So much for the mechanics of the rosary, but the importance of the prayer is that it is a means of drawing closer to God through meditating on details of the Gospels. So the rosary is in three parts, or mysteries: joyful, sorrowful and glorious. The joyful mysteries are the annunciation, the visitation (that joyful meeting of two mothers-to-be), the nativity, the presentation of the infant Christ in the temple and the finding of the boy Jesus in the temple. The sorrowful mysteries take the believer through the passion of Christ, his prayer in the garden of Gethsemane, his scourging and being crowned with thorns, his path along the Via Dolorosa, falling beneath the weight of the cross, and finally the crucifixion. The rosary finishes with the glorious mysteries, of which the first three are biblical: the resurrection, the ascension and the descent of the Holy Spirit. The last two steps in this mystery are the assumption and the coronation of the Virgin Mary.

So we can see that the rosary is a means of prayerful meditation on the life, death and resurrection of the Lord Jesus and a great source of comfort for many Christians. Although for many it seems the sort of prayer which demands time and concentration, in fact, keeping a rosary in your pocket and fingering the beads during the day may be a means of prayerfully staying in the presence of the Lord, because the focus is on the Gospel passages woven through each of the three mysteries and not on any mechanical kind of counting.

For example, a friend tells me that the fifth part of the joyful mystery, finding Jesus in the temple, is a very great anchor for her which, as she puts it, 'seems to reflect the needs of the world and our own spiritual path'. She adds, 'We often "lose" Jesus – or feel we can't find him, even temporarily. Then there are all the many people in the world who have never found him – and the many who for so many reasons have lost him and are lonely and astray. I love this decade of the rosary because Jesus is found, and this is helpful, especially when my faith is dim.'

But even finding Jesus doesn't clear up all the puzzles. In the Bible passage, Jesus responds to his mother with a question which points beyond himself to God: 'Why is it that you sought me? Did you not know that I must be about my Father's business?' (Luke 2.49).

In his early days at her knee, Miriam had taught her son the Scriptures. Later, in the workshop, above the song of the saw and the stretching out of the plumb line and measuring stick, Joseph would have added to the growing boy's understanding of the law and prophets. And now, as he will do in the parables, Jesus takes the words of everyday life, 'my Father's business' (a play on words, for is this not the duty of every Jewish boy?) and points to God. In these very simple words we see that he is growing in understanding that his 'kingdom is not of this world' (John 18.36).

So now, although he goes back to Nazareth and 'was subject to them', as he was expected to be, we are given to understand that a watershed has been reached. Things are outwardly the same, but inwardly Miriam has had a glimpse of the other-ness of her son. Perhaps, as she patched and mended, her thoughts pricked her mind more than the busy needle the torn cloth, as she pondered what all this might mean. Luke tells us, 'his mother kept all these things in her heart' (Luke 2.51). As we observe her through the Gospel story we shall see that, like ourselves, mother Miriam has to learn to take the long view, not least because we must assume that not long afterwards she was left a widow. Joseph the just, the humble, God-fearing carpenter of

Nazareth, disappears from the pages of Scripture after the episode in Jerusalem.

## The steady pace, not the short sprint

Family life, and the life of faith, both require the stamina of a marathon runner. It is the steady pace which counts, not the short sprint. And this is very tough indeed, because everything about us screams out instant solutions. 'The anti-wrinkle system – in as little as three weeks you could be looking ten years younger', the labelling seduces us. And image is everything!

We are assured of instant result with no sweat. Painkillers promise instant relief. We had instant coffee and now, if we're into religion at all, it's got to be instant too.

But as we follow Miriam through the days of doubt and darkness which follow that visit to Jerusalem, we realize that faith takes the long view. To pray, and not to see any results, but to keep on praying; to pray and have your hopes dashed; to pray and feel it's a waste of time; to pray and see it all going wrong – and in Miriam's story what could have gone more wrong? And yet the darkness of Good Friday was not the end for Miriam the mother, as well as for us.

## Prayer is like bread and peonies

Like long-distance running, like hill-walking, prayer is sweat and weariness, it is blisters and grind. The important thing to realize is that it's all right to feel these things. You take body-building food – dried apricots, chocolate – and keep going. So in the marathon of prayer: it's all right to feel angry, even furious, to feel blankness and despair. Keep on going on and sooner or later, as the poet promises, God's smile will 'light a lovely mile'.

As I think of the life of prayer I think of peonies. A friend of mine has called them nature's disasters because their proud crimson heads are so quickly crushed by summer rains, and yet they bloom year after year. They sag and bend – yet bloom.

Dr Janusz Korczak, the children's writer and paediatrician who pioneered the rights of the child in pre-war Poland, felt that the right to believe was basic for children – as basic as bread. Not an adherent of organized religion, Dr Korczak nevertheless recognized the value of prayer and encouraged children in his orphanages to have an act of worship and to pray. Among some of his recently discovered papers was a piece for the Feast of Hanukkah. A little girl asks the festive candle 'What is prayer?' The candle tells her that prayer is just like bread. You get so used to it you don't even think about it. But if you woke up one day and discovered there was no bread you would hunt frantically for even the smallest crumb (Kirchner, 1997, author's translation).

Prayer is a body-building food in the marathon of life. It has often been said that 'the family that prays together stays together'. Family prayer, even if it's only grace round the table, opens the way to forgiveness. It keeps us hanging on. We take it for granted, but without it we starve and fall away. And as we pray we learn our place in the scheme of things: that we are truly loved, that we really matter – but also, as John the Baptist said of himself vis-à-vis Jesus: 'He must increase and I must decrease' (John 3.30).

*Family friction and the way of faith*

# 'For even his brothers did not believe in him' (John 7.5)

Miriam of Nazareth was steadily learning the way of disci-pleship, and her path would take her through the wilderness, for from now on we read of misunderstanding, criticism and strongly negative responses to Jesus within his own home town and among his own kith and kin.

The first episodes occur in Mark 3. Jesus' popularity is growing. Crowds press about him and some people come to 'take charge of him, for they said "He is out of his mind"' (Mark 3.21).

Now, who were the 'people'? Modern English translations render the word as 'his family'. The King James Version says, 'his friends'. Other versions I have consulted have the words, 'those close to him' or 'his relatives'. The Greek original is completely neutral and simply says 'those who were with him'. But just a few verses further on Mark states quite explicitly, 'his brothers and his mother came' and, unable to enter the crowded house, called out to him. This seems to be a separate episode from the one in which people close to Jesus called him mad, but still the division between the eager crowd and the family is made quite clear: 'Then his mother and his brothers came and standing outside they sent to him, calling him' (Mark 3.31–35).

We may be sure that fear of the growing pressure around Jesus and concern for his well-being motivated the family. After all, people were saying publicly, 'he has a demon'. This must have lacerated the mother-heart of Miriam; but a question we have to ask is, were the brothers Miriam's own children?

In many cultures the name 'brother' or 'sister' is loosely

used and extended out to include close kinsfolk. There are instances of this in Scripture, too. In Genesis 13.8 Abram says that he and his nephew Lot are 'brothers'. My Orthodox and Catholic friends explain that the 'brothers' are actually cousins; or else, referring to the tradition that Joseph was an old man, say that these were Miriam's step-children from Joseph's previous marriage. However, although celibacy was not unknown in the Bible, and Jesus himself was unmarried, the Jewish ideal has always been the blessings of a family. We have already seen the sorrow of Hannah, the shame of Elizabeth, at being childless and their joy and praise when the Lord blessed them with a son. Matthew's Gospel tells us that Joseph did not 'know' his young wife until she had given birth to her first-born son, but the words 'until' and 'first-born' imply that the couple in Nazareth had a normal marriage relationship after the birth of Jesus and that there were other offspring. Moreover, the Gospel writers explicitly use the Greek word for 'brother', not any other looser kinship word. Matthew (13.55) and Mark name some of the family of Jesus: 'Is not this the carpenter, the son of Mary and brother of James, Joses, Judas and Simon. Are not his sisters here with us?' (Mark 6.3).

And Jesus' reply was quite cutting: 'A prophet is not without honour except in his own country, and among his own relatives, and in his own house' (Mark 6.4).

John's Gospel similarly records sharp conflict between Jesus and his brothers. His brothers advise him to go up to Jerusalem for the feast of Tabernacles, or Shelters, a major festival. It is clear that the religious authorities in Jerusalem want to silence Jesus, but even so the brothers tell him, not without a sneer, that if he wants publicity he should get his act together and let everyone see him perform some miracle or other. 'For even his brothers did not believe in him,' adds John (7.5), and these poignant words sum up the tensions and divisions within the Lord's family. And the apostle Paul mentions the Lord's brothers in a verse which shows that wives accompanied their husbands on preaching tours: 'Do we have no right to take along a believing wife, as do the other apostles, the brothers of the Lord, and Cephas?' (1 Corinthians 9.5).

## Do my actions wound the saints?

Must we still tear each other apart? Does it matter if these 'brothers' are sons of Miriam, born after Jesus or not? The picture is quite clear: they are close kin. She is their mother, either by virtue of the extended family or because they are indeed her own; and the conflict between them, together with the danger she knew Jesus to be in, must have been another twist of the sword in her heart.

So should I write that the continuing divisions among Christians must still wound the blessed mother's heart? Catholic and Orthodox readers would agree, but would want me to hold the high view of the Virgin Mary which makes it hard to envisage her within a family circle, mothering, nurturing any other children besides her first-born, whether or not they were her own. And Protestant readers would back off at the idea that what we do on earth affects Mary in heaven. My Orthodox and Catholic friends say, 'We ask our friends on earth to pray for us, so why not ask our friends in heaven?' All Christians embrace the idea of the communion of saints – but we can be a little coy about the implications. Do my actions wound the saints? Or do we bring joy to the angels in heaven, as Jesus says (Luke 15.7)?

I still find the whole concept of saints and angels hard, but as I have got older and my heart has been broken, through the pain I have come to believe in both saints and angels: human angels who appear exactly at the right time and in their compassion and generosity embrace afflicted souls.

Let's thank God for the saints and angels! We all agree that Miriam of Nazareth, who honoured the law and taught her child the Scriptures, who baked bread, carried water, wove cloth and patched worn clothes, was great in the eyes of the Lord God. And she was 'poor of spirit' and thus she is to be numbered among those who are truly blessed (Matthew 5.3).

## '. . . those who enter may see the light'

So, let us linger outside the crowded house with mother Miriam and her family and remind ourselves that we are standing alongside the young girl who humbly took God at his word and bore the Saviour of the world. Luke, who told us of young Miriam, who recorded her song and told of the sword, sets the scene less sharply than Mark. It is put within the context of Jesus' story of the sower and the seed – the word of God and the good soil which bears rich fruit. Jesus tells the parable publicly, but explains the meaning privately to the disciples, taking them away from the 'great multitude' which had 'gathered from every city', presumably seeking shelter inside a house. Here, Jesus explains the parable and adds 'nothing is secret that will not be revealed, nor anything hidden that will not be known and come to light' (Luke 8.17). Whereupon word is brought to him: 'Your mother and brothers are standing outside, desiring to see you' (Luke 8.20). There are no threats, only a longing to see Jesus. The Lord's reply is set beside his comment about the light of faith: 'No one, when he has lit a lamp, covers it with a vessel or puts it under a bed, but sets it on a lampstand, that those who enter may see the light' (Luke 8.16).

So Jesus' words, 'My mother and brothers are those who hear the word of God and do it', can be taken as recognition that they too, like the good soil, have already heard and do obey, that they have already 'seen the light'.

The two final episodes in the Gospels which put Miriam fully on stage both show us that she trusted her son implicitly and followed him right to his death. In the next chapter we shall accompany Miriam to the wedding feast and to the cross.

## To ponder

Family friction does not negate the way of faith. It is the steady pace which counts, not the short sprint. Can we allow the Lord into the edgier, more fraught areas of our lives and relationships and glimpse new depths to the meaning of mercy?

## CHAPTER 8

# *Everything is complete*

<hr>

### No more wine!

At the start of his public ministry, John's Gospel tells us, Jesus is invited to a wedding (John 2.1–12). His ready acceptance shows us something of his generous, outgoing attitude. Perhaps family friends were involved, because he brings his mother and his disciples along too.

The ceremony performed, the feasting might continue for a week. We mustn't imagine that Miriam joined Jesus and his followers at the table. Even today, in Orthodox Jewish weddings women serve and sit separately, with the bride and her female relatives. Perhaps then, sitting among the women, Miriam overheard the shocked, embarrassed whisperings. A dreadful social gaffe had occurred: they had run out of wine.

Determined to save the family from embarrassment, and perhaps with no little maternal pride as well as total faith in her son's ability to respond to this sudden need, Miriam must have caused a stir by leaving the women's tables and going across to the men.

And in doing so she publicly acknowledges her son's authority. Perhaps this is why, when Jesus replies, he addresses her formally, indeed distantly, as 'woman'.

We should remember that Jewish men did not converse

with women – a piece of etiquette which Jesus himself would break. His dealings with women are warm and compassionate. Yet even so, there are only two instances when he addresses a woman by name. The first is Martha of Bethany, the second Mary Magdalene: 'And Jesus answered and said to her, 'Martha, Martha, you are worried and troubled about many things' (Luke 10.41); 'Jesus said to her, "Mary!"' (John 20.16).

I find it helpful to reflect that in Poland it's still quite normal to address even close family, as well as strangers, in the third person: 'Would Father like . . .?' 'Is Mama tired . . .?' 'May I give auntie some more tea?' Indeed, 'Pan' and 'Pani' – literally 'lord' and 'lady' – plus a third person verb is the formal way of saying 'you'.

If this is the grammar of relationships, it is also the theme of folk dance. The further east and south we go in Europe, the more formal are the relationships between women and men. A festival of folk dancing recently bore this out. The young dancers from Poland, Czech Republic and Ukraine showed coy but humorous relationships between the sexes: girls playing hard to get, boys leaping in great gyrations and doing amazing things with wooden sticks and mountaineers' axes, but then all coming together again, happily paired off in their colourful regional costumes. But the dancers from Bulgaria, and even more from Macedonia, moved separately and formally to music which to my untutored ear at least was far more oriental. The young men and women did not touch or take hands.

But even so, the term 'woman' as Jesus uses it here is distant and austere. Some Bible versions soften it by prefixing it with 'dear'. Basically, the Lord's reply to his mother seems to be a rebuke: 'It's none of my business.' Yet this is out of keeping with the warmth and generosity we believe to be Jesus' character, as it must have been Miriam's also.

But he explains, 'My hour has not yet come' (John 2.4). Once again he is giving her to understand that his mindset must be upon the will of the Father. Despite the domestic setting of a wedding, Jesus has moved beyond the demands of his human family. It must have taken great faith for Miriam to proceed after she has heard her son's negative, but her humility and complete submission to the will of the Lord underlies her words to the servants, 'Do whatever he tells you' (John 2.5, GNB). The simple words sum up a life of faith. And Jesus works his miracle and changes water into wine.

## Nor can she sue in vain . . .

Formal and solemn, the scene could have been set in a royal court in days of old. Once again, we are reminded of the icons and of a style of worship in which there are no short cuts or abbreviations. In a collection of stories which he wrote in 1912 after visiting Russia and meeting Tolstoy, the poet Rainer Maria Rilke recounts a dialogue between himself and a neighbour, a man too lame to walk or stand:

'. . . all the ceremony, for instance. You speak to the Tsar as you would to God.'

'Oh, so you don't say, "Your Majesty"?'

'No, you call them both "Little Father".'

'And you kneel to them both as well?'

'You throw yourself down before both of them, touch the earth with your forehead and weep and say, "I am a sinner, forgive me, Little Father." We Germans, seeing that, call it unworthy slavery. I think differently about it. What does kneeling signify? It is meant to express reverence. But you can do that well enough by uncovering your head, a German would say. Well, yes – raising your hat, bowing – they are also in a way expressions of it, abbreviations that have come about in those countries where there was not so much room that everybody could throw themselves on the ground. But abbreviations we soon use mechanically, no longer aware of their meaning. That is why it is good, where there is still room and time to do so, to write the gesture out in full, the whole beautiful and weighty word: reverence.'

'Yes, if I could, I too would kneel down,' mused the lame man. (Rilke, 1932)

As we contemplate the formal exchange between Jesus and his mother, we can think back, too, to Queen Esther, the beautiful young girl who risked her life in order to intercede for her doomed people – and averted a pogrom: 'I will go to the king, which is against the law; and if I perish, I perish!' (Esther 4.16).

The Anglican divine and Christian poet John Donne, who said that 'all that Christ did or suffered, concurred to our salvation', wrote in 'The Litanie':

> For that fair blessed Mother-Maid . . .
> Our zealous thanks we pour.
> As her deeds were her helps,
> So are her prayers;
> Nor can she sue in vain
> Who hath such titles unto you.
>
> (Warner, 1999)

At the wedding feast in Cana, mother Miriam did not sue in vain. She lays the need before her son and leaves him to do what he will. Herein is the secret of power in prayer: not clinging to my solutions, but naming the need and leaving the Lord to work things out in his way. If we learn only this from mother Miriam, we shall have learnt much. We cannot make claims on God and, indeed, we see that Miriam has to learn to let go of any claims on her son as a mother and love him and follow him as her Lord. In this she is a model for us all.

## Her son's wedding garment

Miriam's faith and trust are rewarded. Wine is poured out in abundance – and not any old plonk either! The best wine of all, the happy bridegroom realized. But, says John, the source was a secret: only the servants who had drawn the wine from the water jars knew what had happened. Feasting and wine in abundance are signs of the messianic age. Jesus left them to draw their own conclusions. The wedding feast at Cana in Galilee echoes the joyous invitation of Isaiah 55.1: 'Come, buy and eat. Yes, come buy wine and milk without money and without price'. And Amos, the prophet of social justice, predicts, 'The mountains will drip with sweet wine, and all the hills shall flow with it' (Amos 9.13).

Perhaps as Miriam, the woman of faith, learns to stand back and let her son work out his own path, she realizes at that bridal feast that she, too, through her nurture and prayers, has been weaving her son's wedding garment, the cloth of his manhood. Now he must go and meet the betrothed: he is the lover of the Song of Songs and his

darling awaits in the green pastures of Judah, in the valleys
of Galilee . . .

There are six water jugs and six outpourings of the very
best wine of all. God has revealed his glory and the disciples
believed (John 2.11). But when the Son's hour comes, the
new wine of the kingdom will be poured out of the sev-
enth cup, the cup of completion, of suffering and salvation.
Miriam will be there with her son in the suffering of a
death so cruel that it was later banned as a form of execution. Not understanding, not knowing the final outcome,
Miriam is found in the place of discipleship: the foot of the
cross. She is also the mother who stands by helplessly as her
child suffers – and this is the worst pain of all. The sword
Simeon prophesied has twisted in her heart many times
during the ministry of Jesus, but it pierces her altogether
now.

## Don't despair – the end is sweet

> On Friday, mother – do not cry!
> I shall be nailed on wood to die.
> Sharp nails will pierce my hands and feet.
> Don't despair – the end is sweet.

This medieval German poem is representative of a great
devotional outpouring in verse and prose in the wake of
writings by Anselm, Bernard of Clairvaux and the
Franciscan, St Bonaventure. In England in the first half of
the thirteenth century, Edward of Abingdon, Archbishop
of Canterbury, sensitive to a new feeling of devotion for
the cross, desired monks and nuns to meditate on the
passion. Golgotha became the here and now as ordinary

people thought themselves into the drama – and, indeed, Christian drama has its roots in this new spirituality.

There is great emotional identification with Christ – and also with his mother.

## I have put on the crown of the kingdom

Very early Christian art and literature, however, focused on the victory rather than the pain of the passion. The earliest English poem, the *Dream of the Rood*, portrays Christ as a young warrior, a hero who willingly mounts the cross. Within this tradition is an ancient Coptic hymn Christ is said to have sung to his disciples: 'Rise up, O holy Cross, and lift me, O Cross. I shall mount upon you, O cross. They shall hang me upon you as a witness to them. Receive me to yourself, O Cross. Amen. But be joyful, O Cross. Amen. I have put on the crown of the kingdom' (Bennett, 1982).

The emphasis is on triumph and victory. But by the eighth century, a portrayal of the crucifixion in St Catherine's monastery, Mount Sinai, shows Christ with his eyes closed in death. Contemporary with this icon, the spectacular stone cross at Kildalton on the Isle of Islay, carved in the eighth century, when the Norsemen were harrying the west and had already laid waste to Iona, depicts the enthroned mother with her child on the shaft of the cross. They have contemplated over a thousand years of the ebbing and flowing of the tide. They are represented very much in the style of the art of Byzantium and of beautiful early eighth-century frescoes uncovered on the walls of a ruined church at Faras, the ancient kingdom of Nubia, in the valley of the Nile.

The art of Byzantium is also the first to represent the

virgin and St John at the foot of the cross. These two onlookers, the mother and 'the beloved disciple' John, are shown beside the cross in Anglo-Saxon illuminated psalters – their first portrayal in art in England. Soon the virgin and John would be carved on rood screens high above the worshippers in new stone cathedrals. The sufferings of Christ are reflected in the dejected portrayal of the two bystanders, and it was this addition of grieving friends which was to awaken the deeply personal strand in medieval devotion.

## Christ – our chum

I think it is important to understand the changing aspects of spiritual awareness, because they have overwhelmed biblical Miriam. They have influenced our changing understanding of her son, too. Some recent trends have been to make Christ our psychoanalyst and counsellor. Or else, our chum. In the 1950s it was fashionable to explain the miracles in terms of scientific happenings. In the 1960s we had the 'death of God'; in the 1980s the resurrection was denied . . . and so on. And while the Middle Ages imprisoned the Lord in stained glass windows, the market economy packages Christ for a new millennium.

## My God, why have you forsaken me?

Yet how can crucifixion ever be packaged? The naked body nailed to a wooden gibbet and left to die in torment was too much for the disciples, who are conspicuous by their absence that first Good Friday. But the women are there, among the mockers and the drunks; and Miriam is among them. Let us gather up the references in the Gospels. Matthew names the women only at the end of his crucifixion account. He says: 'And many women who followed Jesus from Galilee, ministering to him, were there, looking on from afar. Among them were Mary Magdalene, Mary the mother of James and Joses, and the mother of Zebedee's sons' (Matthew 27.55–56).

'Mary the mother of James and Joses' is, we have seen, Miriam the mother of Jesus. None of the Gospel writers, except John, ever names her as the Lord's mother. Matthew doesn't state any kinship between 'the mother of James and Joses' and 'the mother of Zebedee's sons', but Mark names her: Salome. The evidence suggests that she is the sister of Miriam of Nazareth, the aunt of the Lord. James and John 'the beloved disciple' were therefore Jesus' first cousins (Mark 15.40). Mark also mentions that 'many other women' had come from Jerusalem – and perhaps one of them was his mother, whom we have seen was also called Miriam, or Mary, in whose house the Last Supper may have been held.

## This is the meaning

Notice that the women are 'looking on from afar'. Perhaps that is the closest any one of us can get to the ultimate dereliction of the cross, but the truth is that if we stay with the women, and contemplate the death of the man from Nazareth, Miriam's son, Yeshua, the Christ, we shall be helped to confront our own. We will be drawn into the 'mystery of mysteries': that this, and nothing else but this, is what it is all about. This is the meaning, this twisted body dying on twisted wood beneath dark and lowering skies. This last cry of dereliction in the accents of Galilee, 'Eloi,

Eloi, lama sabachthani' is the only answer to all our questions about suffering and pain.

Miriam the mother heard her son cry out in his native language, and if the curtain within the temple was rent in two, so too must she have been, to the depths of her being.

## Woman, behold your son

John's account mentions four women at the cross: 'His mother, and his mother's sister [unnamed], Mary the wife of Clopas, and Mary Magdalene' (John 19.25). John places himself, the unnamed 'disciple whom Jesus loved' alongside the women beside the cross, and indeed they must have been close enough to hear the Lord's last wishes for his mother. 'Woman, behold your son.' And, 'Son, behold your mother.'

Why did he give his mother into the care of his young kinsman when it is clear that she had sons (or close male relatives) of her own? One suggestion is that the brothers of Jesus were too poor to care properly for their widowed mother – and that this very poverty might have been the reason for some of the resentment they felt that Jesus, the eldest son, who should have been the breadwinner, had made their lives even harder when he forsook the carpenter's workbench.

Another reason was, as John has already told us, the Lord's brothers did not believe in him. Like the other male disciples, they are conspicuous by their absence at the foot of the cross. But his mother was there, and with his dying breath Jesus showed his concern for her, giving her into the care of her young nephew, the 'beloved disciple' – and giving support to that grieving young kinsman too.

Broken-hearted, they were not alone. They would support and comfort one another.

But giving Miriam into the care of his cousin was a sign that Jesus had moved beyond her for ever. His earthly life was finished. All things were truly completed. That cry from the cross, 'My God, why have you forsaken me?' is, in fact, the opening words of Psalm 22, a psalm which plunges through despair to a joyful faith. In the same way, beyond the cross is the resurrection and the risen Lord will return with scars which he will invite Thomas to feel (John 20.27). It is as though he challenged the doubting disciple, 'Touch these scars. Confront the thing you fear. I shrank from suffering, but I went forward to meet it just the same . . .'

> . . . mast and plough are made
> from this felled and damaged tree
> whose canticle awoke the sun.

> Now wood and worker, wound and world are one.

The damaged tree was the cross whose 'canticle' would sing beyond the darkness until it 'awoke the sun'. Then wood and worker, wound and world would all be one.

Miriam could not know this as, with the other grieving women, she laid out the mangled body of her son and tucked fragrant oils and the wild herbs of Galilee into the folds of his shroud. There was no time to embalm the body, for the sun was setting and the Sabbath was about to begin. As soon as it ended the women would set to work on their last act of sorrowing love, preparing the spices with which to embalm the body.

They would work all night, and very early in the morning, while it was still dark, they would go secretly to the garden, their hearts as heavy as the great round stone which covered the entrance to the tomb. 'Who will roll it away for us?' they wondered, but continued on their mission nonetheless.

And found the stone rolled back. The tomb was empty. There was no body to embalm.

Did Miriam understand, even then, what had happened? Gradually the tremendous, mysterious truth dawned, as Jesus appeared to his disciples, family and kinsfolk as risen Lord and Saviour. Brother James was one of those who witnessed the risen Lord (1 Corinthians 15.7). He would become one of the leaders in the Church in Jerusalem (Acts 12.17; Galatians 1.19). But no one can claim blood ties now. There is a new family of faith and it is into this new family that his brothers, believing at last, will be drawn.

We have come to the upper room in the home of John Mark's mother. It is the eve of Pentecost. They crowd in here, the fishermen and the women, the kinsfolk of Jesus and his friends. Former misunderstandings are forgotten as they meet together to pray for the coming of the Holy Spirit, just as the Lord had told them (Acts 1.4).

Can we leave them there? No, of course not. For the Day of Pentecost will dawn and they will be scattered to the ends of the earth. James the brother of John will be beheaded, as Jesus had predicted: 'You will indeed drink from my cup', he had said (Matthew 20.23). He had foretold Simon Peter's death too: 'When you are old, you will stretch out your hands, and another will gird you and carry you where you do not wish' (John 21.18). The challenge is there for all of us as it was for Simon Peter. 'Follow me.'

But what about Miriam, the mother? What about the other women, particularly Mary Magdalene, who played such a prominent part in the resurrection stories? They fade into silence. And where the Bible remained silent, tradition wove its own stories, and 2,000 years of Christian art, literature and devotion have added the rest. In the appendix I have included a list of the councils of the Church and the main festivals in the Church's year. Church tradition has crowned our simple Miriam and clothed her in rich garments, but we perceive her lit with secret joy, as she was when the angel came:

> Amidst gossip and innuendoes
> she walks from hearth to well.
>
> These days there's a look about her
> as if she saw fire and feathers
> flash through cloudy skies.
>
> The wind billows her woven skirts.
>
> A joy she dare not tell
> lights candles in her eyes.

Miriam of Nazareth had cradled her child while armies marched along the high roads of her conquered country and the flare of torches heralded the approach of soldiers with drawn swords. She had followed her son to the foot of the cross and her heart had been broken as she had watched him laid into a grave. But her story – and ours – does not end there. Caught up in the joy of the resurrection, she belongs to the family of faith.

Let us leave her now, as the Lord left her, in the care of John, the beloved disciple. She is growing old, but young and old alike visit her, begging her to tell them about her son. One, dare we suggest, is a young man called Luke, a non-Jew. But Miriam is learning that the family of faith is wider than she had guessed. And Luke wants to know everything about Jesus. Every single thing. And so mother Miriam smiles. She is wearing the black scarf of widowhood and her face is furrowed, but her eyes twinkle as she says, 'Well, you know, it happened like this. I was betrothed to Joseph the carpenter in Nazareth and then, one day, the angel came . . .'

## To ponder

Power in prayer is not clinging to my solutions, but naming the need and leaving the Lord to work things out in his way. We have followed Mary of Nazareth to the end of her journey – have we, too, found that the family of faith is wider than we guessed? Have we found signposts to help us on our way?

# Councils and festivals

As the early Church gradually separated itself from Judaism, and the canon of Scripture as we have it today was put together, various church councils were called to sort out dogma, producing lasting controversy between Eastern and Western Christians. Moreover, as the Church lived out its faith in the pagan world, with its plethora of gods, serious questions arose about Jesus. Was he God or was he just a man?

In 431, a church council met at Ephesus, the city associated with the cult of the goddess Diana, or Artemis (Acts 19.24–40). So perhaps it is significant that it was precisely at Ephesus that the church council decided that, since Jesus is truly God, the mother who bore God in her womb should be called *theotokos*, the God-bearer, the Mother of God.

Nestorius, the Archbishop of Constantinople, had argued that Mary should be called *Christotokos*, the Christ-bearer. But he was outvoted. The title Mother of God, it was thought, would safeguard the divinity of Jesus, who might otherwise be felt to be less than God. So out of the thorny debates of the theologians was born a concept of Mary which places her far above the restraint of the Evangelists. Yet suppose Nestorius had won? Many Reformed Christians would probably have been happier with Mary as 'Christ-bearer'. But then we would have hassles explaining the very thing the council was trying to defend: placing a human Son beside a divine Father. But if the theologians could have foreseen the bloodshed and bitterness which was going to ensue, they might have packed their bags and gone home, leaving the whole issue open.

However, many scholars and Bible researchers argue, the theologians were also responding to a popular need for a cult to replace that of the goddess, whether Diana or Isis or the powerful goddesses of the Celtic world. The first churches to be dedicated to Mary were built around this time, often on the foundation of temples dedicated to pagan deities. She is shown enthroned and crowned, holding her infant son.

We have to realize that, although early Christian art shows Jesus young and beardless as a Good Shepherd, after these church councils Christ is depicted regally clothed in the garb of the emperors and, later, of feudal kings. The crown of thorns makes its appearance quite late in Christian art, only in the thirteenth century, along with the devotion to the suffering man of sorrows.

And along with all this went the promotion of virginity and celibacy as Christian ideals, together with the whole theme of courtly love. Indeed, the differences between Eastern Orthodox and Roman Catholic concepts of Mary are also here, for the art of courtly love, the lady exalted above her lover-knight, did not reach Russia or Greece.

I think it is important to note these differences. In Eastern Orthodoxy Mary is never venerated for herself and she is never shown on the icons alone. She is honoured as the mother of Christ, who is God; she is always shown with her son. His infant hand is raised in blessing. Hers invariably points to him. At every Orthodox wedding the bridegroom is given an icon showing Christ the All-Powerful, one hand raised in blessing, the other holding an open Bible, for he is the living Word. The bride is given an icon of the God-bearer with her child.

Catholicism is less restrained. The reactions to this made the Protestant Reformers, particularly the Calvinist ones, throw the mother out with the bathwater. In Anglicanism she gradually, and rather coyly, found her way back. Then, as a reaction to the severe Protestant position, the Counter-Reformation whirled the virgin even higher and the doctrine of the bodily assumption and the immaculate conception of the Virgin Mary were proclaimed by the popes of the day in 1854 and 1950.

All these developments have brought deep division to Christian Churches, and made Protestants so, dare I say it, chary of Mary.

In order to see where we are today, let's list the Marian festivals in the Church's calendar: Eastern Orthodox (EO), Roman Catholic (RC) and Anglican (Ang).

| | |
|---|---|
| 1 January | (RC) Naming, circumcision of Christ; also the Feast of the Holy Mother of God. |
| 2 February | (EO, RC, Ang) The Presentation of Christ in the Temple, called in the Book of Common Prayer (BCP) the Purification of the Virgin Mary. The old name was Candlemas, and the date coincided with a pagan festival celebrating the lengthening light of approaching spring. In Orthodoxy the Presentation is called |

the Meeting of our Lord and God and Saviour Jesus Christ; in other words, the first public appearance of Christ to his believing people.

| | |
|---|---|
| 19 March | (RC, Ang) St Joseph of Nazareth, Husband of the Blessed Virgin Mary. |
| 25 March | (EO, RC, Ang) The Annunciation of the Most Holy Mother of God and Ever-Virgin Mary was first mentioned as a feast in 692. |
| 24 May | (RC) Most Holy Virgin Mary, Helper of the faithful. |
| 31 May | (RC, Ang) The Visit of the Blessed Virgin Mary to Elizabeth (Anglicans may choose an alternative date for this festival, on 2 July). |
| The Monday after Pentecost | (RC) The Feast of the Most Holy Virgin Mary, Mother of the Church. |
| 26 July | (RC, Ang) Saints Joachim and Anna, parents of the Blessed Virgin Mary. |
| 15 August | (EO, RC) The Assumption of our Lady; The Dormition, or Falling Asleep of our Most Holy Lady the Mother of God. Tradition says that Mary's death took place in Bethlehem in the presence of all the apostles, who were miraculously summoned to her house on clouds. Christ appeared with a host of angels and called to his mother, who looked up and saw him in glory. She blessed the apostles and died, and her soul was then received by her Son in heaven. All this is depicted |

on the icon connected with this major festival. It should be noted that in the Orthodox tradition, unlike the Roman Catholic, Mary dies and does not ascend bodily to heaven; however, an apocryphal story adds that Mary's body rose from the grave and angels carried her to Paradise.

| | |
|---|---|
| 8 September | (EO, RC, Ang) Birth of our Most Holy Lady the Mother of God. This celebration began in Jerusalem in the middle of the fifth century. |
| 9 September | (EO) The Virgin Mary's parents Joachim and Anna are honoured. |
| 21 September | (EO) Entry into the Temple of the Mother of God. Also stems from the Church in Jerusalem when the new Church of St Mary, Mother of God, built by the Emperor Justinian, was dedicated in 543. |
| 8 December | (RC) The Immaculate Conception of Our Lady; BCP calls this simply the Conception. |

(Facts and names of Orthodox feasts from Wybrew, 1997.)

In Russia the Feast of the Protecting Veil of the Mother of God is also an important festival, celebrated in October. It commemorates a battle at which the Mother of God cast her veil over the enemy, allowing the Russians to triumph. And on 3 May the Roman Catholic Church in Poland celebrates the Feast of Our Lady, Queen of Poland.

# References

Bennett, J. A. W., *The Poetry of the Passion*, Clarendon Press, 1982.

Bloom, Anthony, *Living Prayer*, DLT, 1999.

Buksbazen, Victor, *Miriam, the Virgin of Nazareth*, Spearhead Press, Philadelphia, USA, 1963.

Cantalamessa, Raniero, *Life in the Lordship of Christ*, DLT, 1992.

*Church Times*, 23 June 2000.

Chaucer, Geoffrey, *The Prologue to the Canterbury Tales*, ed. John Cunningham, Penguin Critical Studies, 1985.

Day, Peter D., *Eastern Orthodox Liturgies*, Irish University Press, 1972.

Haeften, Barbara von, *Aus Meinem Leben*, private memoir.

Jacob of Serug, *On the Mother of God*, tr. Mary Hansbury, St Vladimir's Seminary Press, 1995.

Julian of Norwich, *Revelations of Divine Love*, tr. James Walsh, SJ, Anthony Clarke Books, 1961.

Brother Kenneth, CGA, ed., *From the Fathers to the Churches*, Collins, 1983.

Kipling, Rudyard, *Puck of Pook's Hill*, Penguin, 1995.

Kirchner, Hanna, ed., *Janusz Korczak – Writer, Pedagogue, Thinker*, IBL, Warsaw, 1997.

Mayhew, Henry, *London Labour and the London Poor*, Penguin, 1985.

Piercy, Marge, *The Art of Blessing the Day*, Five Leaves Publications, 1998.

Rilke, Rainer Maria, *Stories of God*, Sidgwick & Jackson, 1932.

Robertson, Jenny, *Praying with the English Mystics*, SPCK, 1990.

Robertson, Jenny, ed., *Touch of Flame*, Lion, 1989.

St John of the Cross, 'The Dark Night of the Soul', in *Poems*, tr. Roy Campbell, Penguin, 1960.

# References

Underhill, Evelyn, *Mystics of the Church*, James Clarke, 1975.

Wansbrough, Henry, *Luke: The People's Bible Commentary*, BRF, 1998.

Warner, Martin, ed., *Say Yes to God*, Tufton Books, 1999.

Wright, David F., 'Mary in the Reformers', in Wright, ed., *Chosen by God: Mary in Evangelical Perspective*, Marshall Pickering, 1989.

Wybrew, Hugh, *Orthodox Feasts of Christ and Mary*, SPCK, 1997.